"*The Hollywood Project* gets to the soul of today's filmmakers and asks critical questions about the process of making spiritual films. Anyone interested in shaping culture through film should begin by reading this book."

—**Roger W. Thompson**, Executive Director, Rocketown of Middle Tennessee

"Anyone interested in the life stories of spiritually-sensitive filmmakers, whether in the Church (Winter, Derrickson, Batchler, Detweiler) or outside of it (McCanlies, Solomon, Linklater), will find this book an engaging read."

—**Robert K. Johnston**, author of *Finding God in the Movies: 33 Films of Reel Faith* (with Catherine Barsotti) and *Useless Beauty: Ecclesiastes through the Lens of Contemporary Film*

"A serious book has finally been written about real filmmakers of faith and spirituality that will inform, challenge and inspire the Church by way of example, to redeem Hollywood and movies rather than retreat from them. That book is *The Hollywood Project.*"

—**Brian Godawa**, Screenwriter, *To End All Wars* and *The Visitation,* and author of *Hollywood Worldviews: Watching Films with Wisdom and Discernment*

HP | THE HOLLYWOOD PROJECT

By Alex Field

A look into the minds of the makers of spiritually relevant films

[RELEVANTBOOKS]

Published by Relevant Books
A division of Relevant Media Group, Inc.

www.relevantbooks.com
www.relevantmediagroup.com

© 2004 by Relevant Media Group

Design: Relevant Solutions
www.relevant-solutions.com
Cover design by Joshua Smith
Interior design by Jeremy Kennedy

Relevant Books is a registered trademark of Relevant Media Group, Inc., and is registered in
the U.S. Patent and Trademark Office.

Unless otherwise noted, Scripture quotations are taken from the HOLY BIBLE, NEW
INTERNATIONAL VERSION®. NIV®. Copyright © 1973, 1978, 1984 by International
Bible Society. Used by permission of Zondervan Publishing House. All rights reserved.

For information or bulk orders:
RELEVANT MEDIA GROUP, INC.
POST OFFICE BOX 951127
LAKE MARY, FL 32795
407-333-7152

International Standard Book Number: 0-9746942-1-5

04 05 06 07 9 8 7 6 5 4 3 2 1

Printed in the United States of America

Dedication

For my wife, Nicole

CONTENTS

THE HOLLYWOOD PROJECT

HP INTRODUCTION

◈ Alex Field

Film is, for better or worse, the twenty-first century's dominant form of popular literature. Like verbal storytelling and the oral tradition, theater, narrative fiction, and music before them, movies dominate our culture's literary landscape almost entirely. I think movies are critical shakers of culture, especially in terms of spirituality and God.

If you're willing to give me a few minutes, I'll explain why.

This book just sort of happened. Literally, I started writing about film-makers (whom I find eminently fascinating), the craft of filmmaking, and the motivations involved for the men and women who regularly tackle mammoth film productions with the goal of making a movie that moves somebody. Filmmakers want their audiences to laugh, cry, smile, or simply relate to the movie they're watching. All films have a purpose, and all filmmakers want their work to resonate in line with that purpose.

Along the way, I discovered that people have written loads about film, video, and the filmmakers themselves; I found books, articles, and web-sites filled with assumptions, judgments, reviews, and a wide range of movie theory. I also found a whole bunch of really great movies that tackled the issue of spirituality, God, agnosticism, forgiveness, or universal truth—films that cracked open a host of spiritual themes and brought their audiences along for the ride. I also watched a lot of poorly made spiritual films, some of which you have probably seen.

Then I made a list.

I wrote down every spiritual film I could think of, explicit or not, Christian or otherwise. I wrote down movies made by non-Christians, atheists, agnostics, and others all over the spiritual landscape. I watched more movies. I read interviews, books, and articles. I researched filmmakers' lives, histories, and influences. I started collecting all these bits and pieces and filing them away for future use.

Somewhere in the midst of all this, I decided that to discover the motivation behind these projects, I would have to talk with the filmmakers themselves. And thus the concept for *The Hollywood Project* was born.

In the visually motivated postmodern world, films and movies are the most innovative form of literature. Film is a creative, engaging, startling, and massively collaborative artistic medium that has harnessed the psyche of mainstream culture. You and I watch movies because we want to experience the jarring thrill of escaping into another's world, if even for a mere two hours.

Historically, the word "literature" was never meant to be limited to just the written word. Interestingly enough, literature is a simple reference to culture. And by definition, literature, or the production of literary work, is a reference to something that embodies the characteristics of learning. In other words, a piece of literature is any form of art or culture that can teach, whether it's a novel, a book of history, a composition of music, a painting, an opera, or in our case, a film.

Of course, if film is the new literature, then the literary minds of our generation are filmmakers: the screenwriters, directors, and producers. If film is creative exploration, then filmmakers are the explorers.

In this book, I am not interested in counting bad words, classifying sex scenes, deconstructing violence, or categorizing either the films discussed or the filmmakers. If you're looking for a book with a list of clean films to watch in church or in a small group, you might be surprised when we discuss the merits of *Hellraiser: Inferno*. But I urge you to read on. I will not always answer the questions I pose, but I will always ask questions worth considering.

It is important to note that throughout this book, I will quote filmmakers from a variety of sources, including books, magazines, and newspapers. But if you come across direct quotes from the filmmakers themselves without a footnote or cited source, I have either gathered that quotation in a personal interview or while listening to the filmmaker speak in person.

When I first embarked on this project, my goal was very simple. I wanted to hear directly from the filmmakers themselves about their original intentions, their spiritual ideals, and what they've learned about God and film. One question constantly beat in my head like a drum: How can we truly change culture through film?

This isn't a question to dismiss quickly. The truth is that every day, films are changing people's minds, stirring up controversy, unearthing compassion for various causes, and inspiring people to make big decisions that ultimately change their lives.

In his book, *Eyes Wide Open: Looking for God in Popular Culture*, William Romanowski said, "To argue that popular art reflects society is to oversimplify what is really a complex process. In the course of representing or portraying our lives and culture, the popular arts popularize and glamorize the ideals, values, attitudes, and beliefs that exist within our culture. In this way, the popular arts contribute to the power of culture to shape lives. The popular arts reflect a culture they help create."[1] In Romanowski's evaluation, film mirrors culture while at the same time shaping, molding, and creating it. If this is true, then cinema is a self-perpetuating force of creative power that we as Christians cannot ignore.

As you will read, the other unifying theme of this book is this question: How can Christians make more powerful spiritual films or make a significant difference in the Hollywood ranks? In attempting to discover the answer, I interviewed numerous filmmakers from across the spiritual spectrum. I interviewed Christian filmmakers who are out there right now making better films—some of their films are spiritual; some not. I also interviewed a handful of non-Christian filmmakers who have explored spiritual issues or excelled in making culturally significant films that display elements of excellence from which Christian filmmakers can learn.

Again, the only way to really understand the differences between what some Christian filmmakers are doing now and what Hollywood is doing quite a bit better, is to speak with the people behind the cameras.

For too long, Christians have been judging film through a narrow moral lens that forsakes the value of aesthetic excellence while dismissing the reality of the world we live in and the true spiritual searching in which our culture is engaged.

In Paul Thomas Anderson's ensemble masterpiece *Magnolia*, we find many examples of bitterness, anger, immoral sex, and real people in sinful situations. Surprisingly, when the film ends, we're struck with seven or eight redemptive moments of genuine compassion and forgiveness. I think of the powerful scene in which Jim Curring (John C. Reilly), the police officer, delivers the film's final monologue while driving in his patrol car, summarizing the theme of the entire film in a moving speech to himself. Curring speaks as though he's on the television show *Cops*, describing his life and his job even though no one is there to listen. He says, "I have to take everything and play it as it lays. Sometimes people need a little help. Sometimes people need to be forgiven. And sometimes they need to go to jail. And that is a very tricky thing on my part, making that call. The law is the law, and heck if I'm gonna break it. But if you can forgive someone, well that's the tough part. What can we forgive? Tough part of the job. Tough part of walking down the street."[2]

I was struck by *Magnolia* the first time I saw it, but I was torn by the fact that I didn't know where the filmmaker was coming from in his depiction of forgiveness. Can we simply push this film aside, despite its realistic though worldly portrayal of forgiveness—a theme that is at the heart of everything Christianity stands for?

Robert K. Johnston talked about the dilemma of receiving spiritual truth from non-Christians, and specifically *films* made by non-Christians, in his book *Reel Spirituality: Theology and Film in Dialogue.* "Christians need not claim that non-Christian filmmakers are covert Christians or simply appropriate from their movies what is congenial to or congruent with their understanding of the Christian faith," Johnston wrote. "Rather, if viewers will join in community with a film's storyteller, letting the movie's images speak with their full integrity, they might be surprised to discover that they are hearing God as well. If this sounds surprising, it is no more so that Assyria was once God's spokesman to Israel."[3]

I believe we need to be open to the spiritual truths and even spiritual critique that comes from non-Christian filmmakers and their films, including Paul Thomas Anderson's compelling portrait of forgiveness, though he may not hail from a Christian worldview.

Finally, I hope to sufficiently outline the defining characteristics of some of the more spiritually relevant films that are making people think seriously about God and the purpose of their lives. As you read about various screenwriters, directors, and producers, I will identify the specific elements of their films that increase the spiritual depth or excellence of their films.

A new generation of filmmakers is readying itself to tell some powerful stories that will mirror culture while at the same time creating it. And on that note, I'm wondering who you are.

Let me take a brief stab at this. I think you like watching movies. Maybe you simply want to think, watch, or write more critically about God and film. Maybe you are a screenwriter, writing sprawling epic movies about something of great importance in your life. Maybe you are a director or producer of crazy little independent movies and you want to take the next step. You might be a combination of all of these. You are in good company.

Wherever you fall on this spectrum, the filmmakers interviewed here have many stories to tell. I hope you enjoy the ride as much as I did.

Alex Field

NOTES

1. William D. Romanowski, *Eyes Wide Open: Looking for God in Popular Culture* (Brazos Press, Grand Rapids, MI: 2001) p. 32.
2. Paul Thomas Anderson, *Magnolia* (New Line Cinema, 1999).
3. Robert K. Johnston, *Reel Spirituality: Theology and Film in Dialogue* (Baker Academic, Grand Rapids, MI: 2000) p. 72.

HOLLYWOOD project
FILMOGRAPHY

01 MEL GIBSON

THE PASSION OF THE CHRIST

"I've had a few dry [showings of *The Passion of the Christ*] with secular audiences to get an honest response from people. Usually believers are kind of quiet, but this audience wasn't like that at all. [When the movie was over], they were literally on their feet cheering. It had kind of God-smacked them." —Mel Gibson

After Mel Gibson's *The Passion of the Christ* hit theaters on February 25, 2004 (and hit them very hard), the media firestorm surrounding the film's supposed anti-Semitic portrayal of Jewish leaders more or less died down.

But the media coverage of the film didn't lighten in the least. In fact, it picked up as the film slammed into its first weekend with a massive box office take. The independent film, which was produced for $30 million, took in an estimated $26.5 million on its first day alone.

The majority of the critics who had disparaged the film were quieted by the masses storming theaters, keeping *The Passion of the Christ* at the helm of the box office for three weeks straight. Then after a few weeks in the middle of the field, falling into second place and then third place, *The Passion of the Christ*'s run seemed finished. Then, in something completely unmatched in box office history, *Passion* took in another $17 million on Easter weekend and regained the number one spot again nearly eight weeks after it opened. "That's unprecedented. I've never seen that before. *The Passion* is just rewriting box-office history," said Paul Dergarabedian, president of box office tracker Exhibitor Relations. "This movie is tailor-made for a weekend like this. It's not just a movie. It's a religious experience for many people."[1]

The major studios that had passed on Gibson's unique project were undoubtedly kicking themselves as they watched indie distributor New Market, in partnership with Icon Pictures, rake in nearly $370 million in domestic ticket sales, making *The Passion of the Christ* one of the top grossing films of all time.

All of this was powered by a heavy grassroots media campaign that, for the first time in film history, truly harnessed the power of the Christian marketplace and stirred up a furor that made movie history.

As the controversy grew from a buzz to a roar over the course of 2003, the overwhelming ruling from inside Hollywood had been that *The Passion of the Christ* would probably fail miserably when it hit theaters. Why would people want to see another movie about Jesus? some critics wrote. People even stood outside theaters on opening weekend holding signs saying things such as, "Mel Gibson's Passion for Cruci–fiction," while some studio executives, speaking to media outlets on conditions of anonymity, vowed never to hire Gibson or support one of his projects again.[2]

Eighty-five-year-old *60 Minutes* commentator Andy Rooney even called Gibson a "wacko." But in response to Rooney's comments, *60*

Minutes received more than thirty thousand complaints via mail and email—the most ever received by the CBS news program.[3]

Various groups, such as the Anti-Defamation League (ADL) (who hadn't yet seen the movie), reported that the film would portray Jews as the "bloodthirsty, sadistic and money-hungry enemies of Jesus."[4]

But Gibson found that he had many supporters as well.

"Gibson's critics may resent these elements of the drama, but they must blame Matthew, Mark, Luke and John rather than Mel," said Michael Medved, Jewish film critic, radio commentator and president of his own Orthodox congregation. "The film seemed to me so obviously free of anti-Semitic intent that I urged Gibson to show the rough cut to some of his Jewish critics as a means of reassuring them."[5]

Gibson followed Medved's advice and showed the film elsewhere, but the controversy continued to grow, despite Gibson's attempts to quell the uproar. During this time, many commentators and journalists even speculated that Gibson himself had manufactured the controversy as a means for marketing his independent film. Stories in *The New York Times*, the *Los Angeles Times* and *The New Yorker* all slammed Gibson's film and Gibson himself for various reasons, including an endorsement that Icon Pictures had attributed to the pope, which was later categorically denied by a wavering Vatican official.

Regardless of how all this rabid controversy came into being, Gibson responded to his extremely vocal critics in almost every interview he conducted. In his February 17 *Primetime* interview with Diane Sawyer on ABC, Gibson responded to the charges: "Critics who have a problem with me don't really have a problem with me in this film. They have a problem with the four Gospels."

When Sawyer asked him who killed Jesus, Gibson replied, "The big answer is, we all did. I'll be the first in the culpability stakes here. [Jesus] was a child of Israel, among other children of Israel. There were Jews and Romans in Israel. There were no Norwegians there. The Jewish Sanhedrin, and those who they held sway over—and the Romans— were the material agents of his demise."

A few months before the film's international release, Gibson was in-terviewed live at Saddleback Church in Lake Forest, California, after a screening of the film. He had been touring the country to promote the film at similar screenings at churches and conferences with audiences comprised mostly of evangelical pastors and leaders. During this particu-lar interview, in front an audience of more than three thousand, Gibson was asked if he was worried about his career suffering as a result of the movie failing at the box office. Gibson replied simply: "I don't care. It was given to me, and it can be taken away."

Ironically, Gibson used over $30 million of his own money to make The Passion of the Christ, and now, after all is mostly said and done, Gibson's film will have made more than ten times what he put up to make the movie.

THE MAKING OF **THE PASSION OF THE CHRIST**

"Eventually, YOU REALIZE THAT YOU NEED TO CHANGE YOUR LIFE, or it's gonna go down the tubes. It's that point where you go, 'I need help.' [So] I used the wounds of Christ to heal my own wounds."
—Mel Gibson

About thirteen years ago, Mel Gibson hit a roadblock in his life. After becoming one of Hollywood's most successful actors, who made mil-lions for every film he starred in, Gibson broke down. On movie sets and in filmmaking circles, he was a well-known prankster and still is, but back then, he had a wild streak that led him to abuse drugs and alcohol and even to contemplate suicide.

"I was filled with hurts, regrets, and transgressions," Gibson told one interviewer. "I felt wounded by life, but God used my pain as a wake-up call to get my attention. I began praying and meditating on Christ's suffering. Even though I'd heard the story many times, I began to envision what He really went through for us—for me. It reached the point where I just had to get the story out."[6]

After the idea for *The Passion of the Christ* had developed in Gibson's mind for almost a decade, he made plans to make the movie. When Gibson was asked whether he felt called to do this movie, he replied: "Yeah, not just calling, but pushes. I was more afraid of not doing it. But nothing's been very easy on this. It was like bows and arrows, bullets flying. Suit up, you know, put the armor on."

A big inspiration for the film, alongside the four Gospel accounts in the Bible, was the book *The Dolorous Passion of Our Lord Jesus Christ* by Anne Catherine Emmerich, a nun who lived in eighteenth century Germany, who was said to have had intense extended visions about the life of Jesus. "I'm not kidding—the book practically jumped out of the bookshelf at me," Gibson said. "I bought this old library of books with some old tomes in there, and I reached up for a title and pulled it out, and the next one to it fell right into my hands, so I started reading it. That book is the one I'm using for the background of this film."

The book recounts what amounted to two months' worth of visions or visitations and is written in the first-person as though Emmerich herself is standing on the scene of the crucifixion and other events. It's a long-shot source to be sure, but the final film seems drawn almost entirely from Scripture and less from Emmerich's vision.

Gibson also enlisted the help of writer Benedict Fitzgerald to write the script with him. For his part, Fitzgerald felt this was the most important project of his career. "I had come back to my Catholic faith and immediately felt that my entire life was in preparation for this project," Fitzgerald said. "Mel contributed to my returning to my faith. I can now pray un-self-consciously, as a result of working with him. It has been not only a joy, but an education working with him."[7]

When Gibson began searching for funding for the unlikely project based on the last twelve hours in the life of Jesus Christ, many dismissed it as ludicrous. The controversy sprung up around the film early on. Somehow Paula Fredriksen, a Boston University professor, and Sister Mary Boys, a professor at Union Theological Seminary in New York, landed early copies of the script and began making comments in print and on various conference panels, saying that the script was historically inaccurate and anti-Semitic.

The script also had a number of other factors against it. First of all, biblical stories weren't exactly blockbuster material in 2002. The last few films produced on the life of Jesus had been shown on late-night TV, and Martin Scorsese's hugely controversial *The Last Temptation of Christ* hit theaters amid a flurry of protests, bringing in just over $8 million for Universal Pictures. Suffice it to say that the studios were extremely leery of another Jesus project, even one from Mel Gibson.

Gibson reported that the studios didn't show interest in the project prior to seeing the film. Warner Brothers, which had a first-look deal with Icon Pictures, had the first shot at distributing the movie and passed.

"We never wanted to go studio," Steve McEveety, an Icon Pictures partner and the producer of many of Gibson's films, said at a conference in Hollywood in 2003. "We just decided, let's distribute this ourselves. We told our investors, 'Plan on losing your money; we're shooting it in Aramaic.' It's a gamble, but it could take off. It could be huge"—words that many should have heeded apparently.

Part of the reason there was little interest is almost certainly due to the fact that Gibson decided to shoot his actors speaking in ancient languages, primarily Aramaic and Latin. In addition to that, when Gibson pitched the film to potential investors, he said he would release it without subtitles, though he eventually added them.

"My partners and I went searching for a studio to attach to the project, but no one would touch it," he said. "They all said, 'Are you crazy? Why are you doing a Jesus movie in Aramaic?' Obviously, nobody wants to touch something filmed in two dead languages, but I understand, because I would have rejected me too if I heard my pitch."[8]

With all this, the project proposal wasn't an investor's dream. In fact, it was considered by most to be a slightly aloof vanity project, akin to scientologist John Travolta's turn as an alien in scientology founder L. Ron Hubbard's *Battlefield Earth*. It's a valid assumption that when someone is too close to a project, sometimes his or her view of it can be skewed. *Battlefield Earth*, for example, tanked and lost millions.

So investors passed on the project, and studios watched and waited. Nobody committed to the film. Gibson wound up financing the majority of it himself, putting up the $30 million necessary to make his masterpiece.

McEveety said that the studios in general haven't wanted to touch the story of Christ for the last few years. "I think Jesus makes people nervous, and when people get nervous, they get afraid," he told a small audience in Hollywood.

So Icon Pictures went in alone. Producers Bruce Davey and McEveety, Gibson's partners at Icon, began scouting for locations, immediately deciding against shooting in Israel. Eventually, they decided to shoot in Italy, in the southern city of Matera, where the legendary Cinecitta Studios are located. Cinecitta has been the site of many major film shoots, including Martin Scorsese's 2002 favorite *Gangs of New York*.

When casting started for *The Passion of the Christ*, obviously there was one role that would make or break the movie: the role of Jesus. From the beginning, Gibson had a hunch about an actor named Jim Caviezel. As Gibson told the story, McEveety went to meet with Caviezel at Malibu's beachfront eatery Neptune's Net to talk about a surfing movie. Gibson showed up at the meeting a bit later, and the two began to chat.

Later, Gibson called Caviezel to offer him the part of Jesus. "From the moment he asked me, I thought, Oh man, do I take the plunge? Half of me wanted to say no. And the other half said, don't think—just react," Caviezel said.[9]

Caviezel, who told journalist Gayle MacDonald that he had been offered the role of Jesus three times before, finally agreed to take the part. "Mel called me back the next day, and almost tried to talk me out of it," said Caviezel. "He said, 'Do you have any idea how hard this is going to be? I've got to tell you, I wouldn't even want to play this.' I said, 'Well, we each have our own cross to bear, don't we?'"[10]

Caviezel is a devout Catholic and a fantastic but little-known actor who has a slate of exceedingly powerful performances under his belt, including turns in *The Thin Red Line*, *Frequency*, and *The Count of Monte Cristo*. The odd thing about the casting decision is that Caviezel's initials are J.C., and when the film was shot, he was thirty-three years old, the same age Jesus was when He died. Coincidence?

"I believe there are no coincidences," Caviezel said. "The fact that Mel came to me when I was still thirty-three years of age, there was a reason. I believe [God] has a great hand in this film. That's why I'm continually asking Mary for help, to show me the perfect way to be her son."[11]

In filling out the rest of the cast, Gibson casted veterans and polished actors, but largely steered clear of major Hollywood stars, except in the casting of Italian actor Monica Bellucci, who had just hit the screen in the two *Matrix* sequels, among other things. In the role of Mary, Jesus' mother, Gibson cast Jewish Romanian actor Maia Morgenstern, who gives a tortured and beautiful performance. In an unexpected move, Gibson then cast a woman named Rosalinda Celentano in the role of Satan. The resulting performance is mysterious and scary, an effect Gibson aimed for and achieved.

Filming began in November 2002 and continued through February 2003 at Cinecitta studios and elsewhere. The sprawling sets, which were created by production designer Francesco Frigeri, re-create the scene authentically, with convincing temples, dwellings, and cobblestone roads. Gibson built a massive set, a replica of ancient Jerusalem, complete with authentic architecture, hundreds of extras, and re-creations of the ancient buildings on two and a half acres of dusty Italian backlot. The enormity of the set itself is astounding to behold, as buildings and houses stretch off into the distance with weathered cobblestone roads winding throughout.

Cinematographer Caleb Deschanel took pains to give the movie a distinct look that mirrored a Renaissance style used by Renaissance artist Michelangelo Mensi da Caravaggio. Gibson asked Deschanel to look to Caravaggio for inspiration when lighting and shooting the film. Apparently, Gibson was pleased when he saw the first few images, saying, "Oh my God. It's a moving Caravaggio!" He went on, bragging to an interviewer about his cinematographer. "This man is a gifted cinematographer, who's probably in the top bracket, right there at the pinnacle with a handful of others."[12]

As for Caviezel's experience playing Jesus, he surely did have his own cross to bear. For starters, his makeup call time was often as early as 2 a.m., especially for the scenes in which Christ is beaten nearly to death. In those scenes, Jesus' flesh is torn, ripped, and flayed in gruesome detail. To achieve the intense special effects, skilled makeup artists and visual effects gurus created thousands of patches of whipped skin to apply to nearly every inch of Caviezel's body, a process that took four to eight hours each day. To allow for long hours of shooting on the cross, a special effects team created a detailed mechanical stand-in of Caviezel's body that was used in many wide and medium shots.

During shooting, Caviezel faced several other extremes as well. He experienced borderline hypothermia after being on the cross for just one day (they shot the cross scenes for more than fifteen days), found himself accidentally beaten several times during the whipping scene, and then got burned from the heaters the crew brought out to counteract the hypothermia. And on top of that, he was even struck by lightning once in front of a group of witnesses, who watched him walk away unscathed.

Caviezel said working on *The Passion of the Christ* has been the greatest lesson of his life and told one journalist that he kept a tiny piece of wood tucked in his loincloth during the shoot—a piece he claims is a relic from the cross on which Jesus actually hung.[13]

Once Gibson had wrapped his film and edited a rough cut, the controversy went into overdrive as he started popping around the country for random screenings. Gibson showed the film to political figures and the top echelon of the media in Washington, D.C., pastors and politicians in New York, critics and pastors in Hollywood, and more pastors and church leaders in Colorado Springs, Colorado. Speculation and controversy quickly became the order of the day.

But after one such screening, liberal Motion Picture Association of America (MPAA) chief Jack Valenti said of the film: "I don't see what all the controversy is about. This is a compelling piece of art. I just called Kirk Douglas and told him that this is the movie to beat."[14]

Unfortunately, Valenti seemed to be in the minority.

Finally, in October 2003, Icon Pictures struck a domestic distribution deal with independent distributor New Market Films, who distributed 2002's powerful *Whale Rider*, along with *Memento* and others. The two companies tried a hybrid distribution model, in which they co-distributed the film domestically. Needless to say, it paid off handsomely.

"Hollywood believed that we couldn't get a distribution deal and that we weren't going to be shown in movie theaters, but we were busily engaging the top three exhibitors nationwide," said Paul Lauer, director of marketing for *The Passion of the Christ*, who estimated some months prior to opening day that the film would open very wide. Speculation in Hollywood was that *The Passion of the Christ* might get into fifteen hundred theaters, a huge number for an independent film.

But on opening day, *The Passion of the Christ* debuted on 4,643 screens in more than three thousand theaters in America alone.

MIRACLES ON THE SET

"We had people from every country, every creed on the crew. PEOPLE WERE REVISITING, RETHINKING, REEVALUATING LIFE; some people were just kind of stunned." —Mel Gibson

In more ways than one, *The Passion of the Christ* is a movie like no other. The film was financed by the director (who happens to be one of the world's best-loved actors), the dialogue is in ancient languages, the distribution model is unconventional, Satan is played by a woman, the story is painstakingly realistic, and also, Gibson brought a priest on-set every morning, offering Latin Mass, communion, and confession for those from the cast and crew who wanted to participate.

Then the assistant director, Jan Michellini, got struck by lightning. Twice. At one point, Jim Caviezel was standing with Michellini under an umbrella on top of a hill. McEveety reported that after they finished shooting a scene, he looked over and saw a bolt of lightning reach down and strike the two men. At a 2003 conference, McEveety said that he saw lightning "coming out of Caviezel's ears." Amazingly, both men were unhurt. Michellini only suffered light burns on the tips of his fingers.

McEveety expanded on the topic of divine intervention in his discussion of the film, describing several small moments where the filmmakers felt that God shined on them on-set. People reported powerful life changes, conversions, and even healings. "Even the craft service guy was affected," McEveety said. "Then there were people praying for the first time in years."

Gibson has also talked about how his diverse international cast and crew got along extremely well, as Christians, Muslims, Jews, Buddhists, and even agnostics worked side by side on the film.

In an interview on the set, Gibson told a journalist, "There have been a lot of unusual things happening—good things like people being healed of diseases; a couple people have had sight and hearing restored. There was even this little six-year-old girl [visiting the set] who had epilepsy since she was born and had up to fifty epileptic fits a day. She doesn't have them anymore, for over a month now. And they really give you a lot of hope. I mean, we're not kidding around about this, it's really happening."[15]

Speaking to a group of pastors about the film, Gibson said, "It was a strange mix of the most difficult thing I've ever done, along with this incredible ease. Everyone who worked on this movie was changed. There were agnostics and Muslims on-set converting to Christianity."

Strange happenings weren't limited to the set either. Once the film debuted in theaters, people reported feeling sick or feeling elated. Marketing director Lauer reported that people were affected in every screening he was a part of, most of which were followed by long, introspective silences.

"This film takes you from the opening sequence where Jesus undergoes His suffering in the Garden of Gethsemene. From that moment until the very end of the film, it grabs you and doesn't let go. People have told me that [they're] experiencing a variety of physical outcomes, including lots of tears. People have headaches, stomachaches. It's a roller coaster; it's physically draining."

Several people even had heart attacks and died during screenings around the country and the world. One man who had rented out several theaters in Argentina died quietly while watching the film; another man who watched the movie felt convicted and later confessed to a murder he had committed.

MEL GIBSON

"IF THE INTENSE SCRUTINY OF MY TWENTY-FIVE YEARS of public life revealed I had ever persecuted or discriminated against anyone based on race or creed, I would be all too willing to make amends. But there is no such record." —Mel Gibson[16]

Mel Columcille Gerard Gibson was born in New York in 1956, the sixth of eleven children. Despite being born in the United States, Gibson and his family moved to New South Wales, Australia, where he was raised and later attended college at the University of New South Wales in Sydney. During college, he began doing theater at the National Institute of Dramatic Arts, something he continued to do after college, along with appearing for a short time on minor TV shows.

But it wasn't until 1979's *Mad Max* that Gibson became an internationally known movie star. That same year, he starred in a movie called *Tim*, for which he won the Australian Film Institute's award for Best Actor. A couple years later, he would win the award again for *Gallipoli*.

Throughout the '80s, Gibson starred in a string of hit films, including *The Bounty*, *The Road Warrior*, *Lethal Weapon*, *Mad Max Beyond Thunderdome*, *Lethal Weapon 2*, and *Tequila Sunrise*. In 1990, Gibson had a big year, starring in two comedies, *Air America* and *Bird on a Wire*, and stunned critics with *Hamlet*, a film that displayed his immense depth as an actor. Gibson's directorial debut, *The Man Without a Face*, wasn't a critical hit, but it was Gibson's personal statement against judging a person by their appearance. Many more films followed, but it was *Braveheart* in 1995, which Gibson produced, directed, and starred in, that would land him two Oscars and a more important spot on the A-list. The powerful film about a Scottish rebel trying to overthrow English rule in Scotland surprisingly did not make a splash at the box office when it was first released into theaters. When the studio re-released the film into the theater twice, toward the beginning of the awards season and toward the end of the box office year, people took notice.

In more recent years, Gibson has made a target of the box office with a number of hits, such as *Ransom, Conspiracy Theory, Lethal Weapon 4, Payback, The Patriot, What Women Want*, and *Signs*.

Gibson was recently ranked number three on *Entertainment Weekly's* annual breakdown of powerful Hollywood luminaries, his movies are consistently box office smashes, and he makes almost as much money as an actor can possibly make in the film business, drawing nearly $25 million for each film in which he stars.

In addition, or perhaps, more importantly, he is also a father of seven and husband to Robin, his wife of nearly twenty-five years. He is also a well-known prankster who radiates energy and maintains a light, relaxed atmosphere on his sets, whether he's acting, producing, or directing.

Gibson was raised in the Catholic faith and now celebrates the Tridentine Latin Mass, an ultra-traditional Catholic service for which he even built a church in Malibu, California. The conservative Catholic group he belongs to rejects the various stipulations stemming from the Vatican II and pays no particular homage to the pope. Gibson returned to the faith after spending much of his thirties in a kind of spiritual limbo.

"I was a pretty wild boy quite frankly," Gibson said of his younger days. "Even now when I'm trying more than I was before, I still fail everyday at some level but that's being human."[17]

Speaking about his upbringing in the Catholic Church, Gibson shared about his perspective on the story of Jesus. "When I was growing up, the whole story of the Passion was very sanitized, very distant; it seemed to me very much like a fairy tale," he said. "Then from about the age of fifteen to age thirty-five, I kind of did my own thing as it were, not that I didn't believe in God, I just didn't practice faith or give consideration."[18]

But during those twenty years, Gibson became an international star, a profession that is a lonely career. "I got to a very desperate place. Very desperate," he told Peter J. Boyer from *The New Yorker* in September 2003. "And I didn't want to hang around here, but I didn't want to check out. But when you get to the point where you don't want to live, and you don't want to die—it's a desperate, horrible place to be. And I just hit my knees. I had to use the passion of Christ to ... heal my wounds."[19]

In the past, Gibson has talked about God's hand in his life, citing a near-fatal car accident he was in while driving through the twisting roads of the Blue Mountains in Australia. Gibson was passing a slow-moving truck when he saw an oncoming truck and swerved off the road, slamming into a tree that saved him from careening off a cliff. He was twenty-one years old at the time. Moments like these gave him evidence of God's hand in his life and also foreshadowed the intense spirituality he exhibited in making and marketing *The Passion of the Christ*.

Gibson has also shown his spiritual side in other films as well. In the 2002 thriller *Signs*, Gibson played a preacher who had lost his faith after the death of his wife. While the spiritual film was one of the keys to Gibson's interest in the role, he said he doesn't think he'll ever lose his faith, because of his fear of God.

"During the course of one's life, one is presented with circumstances that could shake it," Gibson told the Associated Press in August 2002. "I don't think I ever lost it. See, basically, I'm too scared. I'm too scared of getting a lightning bolt up my posterior."[20]

A BRIEF **HISTORY OF CHRIST** ON FILM

"I'VE NEVER SEEN A RENDERING THAT EQUALS THIS for reality. The versions I've seen either suffer from bad hair, inaccurate history, or

not just being real. And somehow, because of that, I think you're distanced from them somehow. THEY'RE MORE LIKE FAIRY TALES."
—Mel Gibson[21]

Jesus Christ is probably the most documented film character, historical or otherwise, in the history of motion pictures. And in the visions of many powerful filmmakers, Jesus has been portrayed in all shapes, sizes, personalities, and skin tones. Perhaps it's appropriate then that Jesus' filmic biography is made up of a long list of films that interpret biblical history in various ways, in effect broadening Jesus' appeal to a diverse world audience.

In 1999, the made-for-TV film *Jesus* was released, sporting a power-ful version of the passion story, featuring an ever-smiling Christ that moved the pope to give it his glowing endorsement, which was later reproduced in its entirety on the film's DVD. And of course, the other well-known film titled *Jesus* is the Campus Crusade evangelistic tool, which is also known as *The Jesus Film*. *The Jesus Film* was touted by its makers as the most accurate portrait of Jesus of its time and has been shown around the world in hundreds of languages. Interestingly enough, an evangelistic message and a reciting of the sinner's prayer follows the movie.

The most controversial attempt (prior to the *The Passion of the Christ*) at the Gospel story was Martin Scorcese's *The Last Temptation of Christ*, which premiered in 1988 and met with scorching criticism from reli-gious leaders, divided reviews, and even massive protests, which came from Christians around the world.

The film, however, is not a scathing denial of Christ's divinity so much as it's an interpretation of Jesus' full humanity. Christians believe Jesus was fully human and fully God as He walked the earth. *The Last Temp-tation of Christ* simply attempts to portray the human side of Jesus' life, though admittedly, the liberties it takes are what garnered the outcry.

The main point of protest is a scene that portrays Jesus while He's on the cross, thinking about what life might have been like if He had married Mary Magdalene and had children instead of sacrificing Himself for the world. While the scene is entirely fictional, it rests on the biblical idea that Jesus was tempted in His life though He was without sin.

After an extended dream sequence, Jesus dies on the cross, giving Himself for the sins of the world. And thus the movie stays on solid footing theologically. But the film drew such a vivid picture of temptation that Christians lashed out at the filmmakers and the studio that released the film. Former Campus Crusade leader Bill Bright was even reported to have said that he would raise $10 million to buy the film so that he could destroy it.[22]

Jesus has seen countless incarnations on celluloid prior to this as well. It is almost as if each generation has come up with its own take on Jesus' life. In the 1980s, *The Last Temptation of Christ* made its mark. The 1970s saw the release of the hippie musical *Jesus Christ Superstar*, along with *Godspell*, *The Jesus Film*, and the fantastic intensity of *Jesus of Nazareth*. In the 1960s, filmmakers unleashed a slew of films about Jesus, including the long and incredibly dull *The Greatest Story Ever Told*, the epic *King of Kings*, and the pseudo-realistic *The Gospel According to St. Matthew*. The 1950s brought us the rousing Gospel epic and eleven Academy Award-winning *Ben Hur* with Charleton Heston. *Ben Hur* was actually a remake of two previous movies of the same name, which were released in 1907 and 1927 respectively. Oddly enough, no literal Jesus film actually hit theaters in the 1990s unless you consider *The Matrix*, with its startling Christ figure parallels, a worthy equivalent. So far, the twenty-first century's first four years have tallied up a massive number of Gospel films, including the recent films *Judas*, *The Gospel of John*, *The God Man*, *The Lamb*, *The Alpha and Omega*, *The Passion of the Christ*, and *Matthew*, among others.

Many other films about Jesus have been made, including *The Robe*, *The Gospel Road*, *Hail Mary*, *The Messiah*, the silent film *From the Manger to the Cross, Mary, Mother of Jesus*, the Monty Python parody called *The Life of Brian*, and the original version of *The King of Kings*. Some critics estimate that the story of Jesus has been committed to film more than a hundred times since film became a massive consumer medium near the turn of the twentieth century.

A **NEW** VISION

"If you look at a lot of Bible movies, they're, you know, they lack reality. [But] I hope this lives on. I THINK IT'S TIMELESS AND I TOLD THE TRUTH as far as I could." —Mel Gibson

Gibson has a short cameo in *The Passion of the Christ*.

Near the end of the movie, Gibson's fist enters the frame clutching an eight-inch iron spike. His hand is only on-screen for a few moments, as it holds the nail being driven through Jesus' palm by a flashing hammer.

"We are responsible, collectively, as the human race, because it was our sins that nailed Jesus to the cross," Lauer said. "And Mel has said that many times. He believes that. In fact, it is Mel's hand that lays the spike in Jesus' hand in the film. That certainly points to the fact that he sees himself, first and foremost, responsible."

The symbolic cameo is a subtle nuance that flies in the face of the flaring controversy over the film's portrayal of Jewish leaders as the people responsible for Jesus' death. Gibson's symbolic cameo spreads the blame more evenly. It's a gesture of humility that acknowledges all sinners as responsible parties in the death of Jesus Christ. It's also another example of how Gibson told this story in a vastly new way.

Gibson talked about what made this retelling of Christ's life fresh and more authentic when compared to previous films about Jesus. "Other versions often suffer from bad hair or stilted acting," he said in response. "I want to make the story real and not portray it as a fairytale."

In another interview, he elaborated. "I don't think other films have tapped into the real force of this story," Gibson told the Zenit news agency. "We've done the research. I'm telling the story as the Bible tells it. I think the story, as it really happened, speaks for itself. The Gospel is a complete script, and that's what we're filming."[23]

But *The Passion of the Christ* isn't just any attempt at tackling the story of Jesus' final hours; Gibson made authenticity the project's top priority. In that spirit, Gibson made the decision to film in ancient languages early on, hoping that he could release it without subtitles. His reasoning for such a strange move actually makes a lot of sense.

"I always wanted to do a Viking movie," Gibson said. He elaborated by saying that if he saw a group of Vikings getting off a boat speaking a rough Germanic language that he couldn't understand, they'd be imposing and scary. "If they get off the boat speaking in a language you understand, they're not scary anymore."

Seeing the dialogue performed in the original languages gives the film an academic kind of weight that is generally reserved for the theater or the opera. The power of the words lends credibility to each character's lines, a depth that stems from the thought that many have had—that this film could reflect more accurately what Jesus might have sounded like or how He might have actually spoken. And this additional element also charges Jesus' words with an incredible power that rivals anything seen before on film.

Though many scratched their heads when Gibson chose to film his script in ancient languages, the dedication to total authenticity won the day. "The decision was made very early in the process," Gibson said. "I want to transcend language with the visual."

Reactions to the film from early screenings were almost unanimously positive. Gibson chose to screen his film for Christian leaders and pastors to get advice and a general impression for how people might react—surprisingly, people almost always reacted with intense, respectful silence. But there have been a wide range of other reactions as well.

Much of this might be attributed to the intensity of the violence. In the spirit of realism, the depictions of Christ being arrested, beaten, whipped, stabbed, spit on, and finally crucified are more graphic than any film about Jesus to date. Gibson pulls no punches, allowing each step of Christ's journey to the cross to resonate on-screen, to settle in the gut of the viewer. Gibson himself has said no one under thirteen should see the film, unless they're especially mature.

In an added twist, Gibson shows Satan in a new way as well. In the movie, this mercurial character comes to life as a striking albino in a dark cloak, haunting Judas before and after his betrayal and shadowing Jesus in certain scenes. Gibson cast a woman in the role.

"The woman we cast is very beautiful," Gibson said. "I didn't want the stereotypical devil with horns. I don't believe that is how the devil presents himself/herself. He/She is very seductive and doesn't put out signposts announcing who he/she is. Evil tends to emulate good, but it's wearing a bad mask."

CONTROVERSIAL **CHRIST**

"Anti-Semitism is not only contrary to my personal beliefs, IT IS ALSO CONTRARY TO THE CORE MESSAGE of my movie." —Mel Gibson

Strangely, *The Passion of the Christ* found itself many critics in March 2003, a full year before its release into theaters, as various activists, journalists, and organizations struck out at Gibson based on an early version of the script that was mysteriously circulated. The Anti-Defamation

League (ADL), the Jewish persecution watchdog, almost immediately became the most vocal of all Gibson's newfound foes, waging a campaign to change various aspects of the script and, subsequently, the film.

The ADL claimed in a statement dated June 24, 2003, that the movie wrongly portrayed Jews in a way that is anti-Semitic and asked Gibson in a largely hostile statement, "Will the final version of *The Passion* continue to portray Jews as blood-thirsty, sadistic and money-hungry enemies of Jesus?"[24]

All of this early criticism was based on readings of an early and supposedly unauthorized script or secondhand reports from a handful of journalists. It seemed apparent that someone, and very soon many people, was intent on stirring up controversy about this movie, regardless of the validity of the claims made.

Protestors identified numerous elements of the film that they disagreed with or were offended by, but the most contentious charge that was launched primarily in Gibson's direction was the charge of anti-Semitism. The charge rested on fears that the film portrayed the Jews as the people responsible for Jesus' death, which could inspire bouts of anti-Semitism.

Talk has always surrounded this film for one reason or another. Even the preproduction and shooting of the film were fertile ground for a barrage of rumors about a number of things, including Jim Caviezel's injuries on-set, the use of ancient languages, or the extreme violence of the film.

The New York Times took the first shot at the film by reporting that Gibson's father, Hutton Gibson, denied that the Holocaust ever took place. Jewish and Catholic critics began to wonder if *The Passion of the Christ* would come from a similar stance and began to stake out their positions.

The media kicked into overdrive around this time, when Fredriksen and Boys claimed to have seen an early version of the script. The women declared that the script contained historical errors that could spark anti-

Semitism or prejudice against Jews. Fredriksen even published an article in *The New Republic* titled "Mad Mel." Neither of the two scholars had yet seen the film.

On top of that, Icon Pictures claimed that the script was stolen, noting that it wasn't the same script that was used to shoot the film. For her part, Boys said an Icon employee gave the script to an intermediary, who relayed it to her.

Either way, her critique of the script made some controversial claims. "For too many years, Christians have accused Jews of being Christ-killers and used that charge to rationalize violence," Boys told an interviewer. "It seems to me that the film looked on Jews as antagonists, Jesus as this perfect victim."[25]

Around the same time, the ADL and the United States Conference of Catholic Bishops gathered a panel of scholars, including Boys and Fredriksen, to review the early version of the script. While the ADL claimed that this panel was gathered with Gibson's blessing, saying Icon "indicated their willingness," Icon maintained its claim that the script was stolen.[26] In late spring of 2003, after they learned that a staff member had obtained the early draft, the U.S. Conference of Catholic Bishops apologized and returned the script.

But despite Icon's protests, the ADL and its outspoken national director Abraham Foxman took no time to slam Gibson's project, criticizing the film and its potential for sparking further anti-Semitism. In their statement, the ADL said, "The screenplay reviewed was replete with objectionable elements that would promote anti-Semitism." The statement went on to ask for a series of changes in the script and the film, criticizing "fictitious non-scriptural elements," "excessive violence," and the "inescapably negative picture of Jews."[27]

The ADL's statement was by turns inflammatory and unprofessional, while asking for things that undeniably violate an artist's freedoms. In

addition, a comparable film that hit theaters only a few months prior
to *The Passion of the Christ* inexplicably didn't face such criticism. *The
Gospel of John*, which hit theaters on September 26 and was released on
video and DVD in November 2003, depicted the same events as Gibson's film, yet received no censure from the ADL or anyone else.
Lauer commented on this inconsistency back in December 2003. "It's
interesting that there are different films out adhering to the Gospels, but
only one is being attacked," he said. "I think fair-minded individuals and
leaders in the Jewish community to whom we have exposed the film
have received it well, and that includes people like Michael Medved."

The fears of the critics are understandable, but they're not warranted,
Lauer went on to say. "When you see a continuing attack, you have to
start wondering whether people are being reasonable or whether there's
an agenda. I think that some groups exist to fight an enemy, and if they
don't have an enemy, they don't have a reason to exist."

Medved has been an outspoken champion of Gibson's film and more
important, his right to make the film his own way. In an article he wrote
for *Christianity Today*, Medved said: "I felt heartsick over the denuncia-
tions of an unfinished movie almost no one had seen ... Could the
recriminations over *The Passion* divide Jews from the Christian conser-
vatives most likely to embrace the film?"[28]

On Medved's recommendation, Gibson showed the film to select groups
of Jewish leaders around the country. The screenings for Jewish and
Christian leaders were also an attempt to assuage the fears generated by
the media frenzy. While Gibson's attempt won over many other Jewish
leaders including radio personality Matt Drudge, others still attacked the
film, resulting in more headlines.

In August 2003, Gibson finally screened a rough cut of the film for
another audience in Houston—one that included ADL official Rabbi
Eugene Korn, who was the director of the ADL's Office of Interfaith
Affairs in New York at the time. Korn told the *Houston Chronicle* the day

after he screened the film, "We still have grave concerns."[29]

The controversy roared on, gaining momentum toward the end of the year. Then in November 2003, Korn resigned his post with the ADL, saying he needed "a more reflective and contemplative environment."[30] The resignation immediately brought up concerns in the Jewish community that the ADL had been too aggressive in dealing with Gibson's film. Jewish scholars and advisers suggested that the ADL might have achieved the opposite of its goal by building a national interest in the film instead of squashing interest, as might have been their intention. Medved agreed with this assessment.

"If the film becomes a hit, the over-wrought Jewish critics of the film will have succeeded only in demonstrating their irrelevance," Medved wrote. "And if the movie flops at the box office and reaches only a limited audience, it can hardly make a significant contribution to anti-Semitism."[31]

Increasingly, as news outlets worldwide covered the story, the blame and the controversy fell upon Gibson himself. And according to Lauer, the controversy hasn't been easy. "No one has come out of the film saying that it inspires hatred toward anyone," Lauer said. "[But Mel's] been living a very difficult life for the last six months. Friends that used to be friends are no longer friends."

Despite the personal nature of the fallout, Gibson showed poise in maintaining his stance, even going so far as to lightly soften the areas of the film that might have been considered offensive. Gibson proved himself to be a director concerned with the theological and historical accuracy of the film by seeking feedback from religious leaders and scholars.

Over the course of the latter half of 2003, Gibson continued to show the film to scores of pastors, priests, teachers, and religious leaders from around the world. Response from the clergy and academia ranged from the slightly critical to complete and unabashed support from leaders such as Ted Haggard, Larry Poland, and Don Hodel.

While the film started to gain momentum and Christian support, Fredriksen and Boys reported that they had been receiving harassing phone calls, hate mail, and numerous emails for their comments against the film. Sadly, other organizations that criticized the film, such as the Simon Wiesenthal Center, also reported receiving hate mail for their comments. This unfortunate display of anti-Semitism confirmed the reality of the ADL's fears—but the harassment came in response to comments made to the press prior to the film's release, not in response to the film itself.

Ironically, the criticism continued to come from people who hadn't seen the film. But Gibson's loudest critic by far continued to be Abraham Foxman, the national director of the ADL. "We were troubled … that it portrayed the Jews, the Jewish community, in a manner that we have experienced historically," Foxman told CNN. "Seeing passion plays used to incite not only a passion of love in terms of Christianity, but at the same time, to instill and incite a hatred of the Jews because of deicide."[32]

Foxman later told *The Washington Post*, "I would like to see the movie, and if it turns out I was wrong, I'll be the first to say so."

Then in January, the *Los Angeles Times* reported that Foxman had not only seen the movie, but he snuck into a Florida screening to do it. Foxman paid a $295 registration fee at a Beyond All Limits Christian conference, listed himself as a member of the Church of Truth, and watched the film. In a statement released later, Foxman said, "*The Passion of the Christ* continues its unambiguous portrayal of Jews as being responsible for the death of Jesus."[33] Gibson's spokesman Alan Nierob, who is Jewish himself, responded by saying, "We respect the right to freedom of expression and expect the same in return."[34]

In the week prior to the film's massive opening, *Passion* fever had engulfed the country. The film drew stories and opinions from every news and media outlet in the country, including unprecedented press coverage in Christian circles. By every estimation, *The Passion of the Christ* would be a hit; there was no longer any doubt that people would storm theaters on the film's opening day.

When Diane Sawyer finally aired her interview with Mel Gibson on ABC only days before the film opened, she included an interview with Foxman to get his final words before the film's release. "I do not believe it's an anti-Semitic movie," he said. "I believe that this movie has the potential to fuel anti-Semitism, to reinforce it." Foxman also said that he doesn't think Gibson is anti-Semitic himself. "This is his vision, his faith; he's a true believer, and I respect that. But there are times that there are unintended consequences."

Then, when it seemed that the controversy was about to die away, another controversy sprung up to take its place just weeks before the film was released. Icon Pictures partner Steve McEveety had given a tape of the film to Pope John Paul II's personal secretary, Archbishop Stanislav Dziwicz, hoping the pope would watch the film. According to Peggy Noonan of *The Wall Street Journal*, Dziwicz reported back to McEveety later with the pope's five-word response to the film: "It is as it was." The story broke and was reported by *Daily Variety*, Reuters, and *The New York Times*, some noting that Icon Pictures had already posted it on their website as part of their marketing campaign.[35]

Then a few days later, after the story had had time to circulate and gain credibility, Dziwicz publicly denied that the pope said any such thing. This development immediately cast both sides into a strange light; either Gibson had manufactured the quotation completely, or the Vatican had gotten nervous when the comment drew international attention and pulled its endorsement with a quick denial. The issue was left at that, never culminating a sure resolution.

Once the film opened, all news seemed to focus on its incredible box office success—until several disconcerting reports began to surface from several Muslim countries. For example, in Bahrain, *The Passion of the Christ* was banned because it was said to be against Islam, which forbids the depiction of prophets such as Jesus or Moses. But Bahrain was the exception.[36]

In countries throughout the Arab world, including Jordan, Syria, Lebanon, and Egypt, where movies like *The Prince of Egypt* were banned because of their depiction of the prophet Moses, *The Passion of the Christ* has been welcomed and wholeheartedly embraced. This is disconcerting because audiences are embracing the film due to its supposed negative portrayal of Jews. In one scary report, one young woman came out of the film with tears in her eyes, saying that the film "unmasked the Jew's lies and I hope that everybody, everywhere, turns against the Jews."[37] These comments come despite the fact that chapter 4, verse 157 of the Koran denies that the crucifixion ever happened. Muslims believe another man was crucified in Jesus' place.

Still, it's interesting to note the fact that the story of Jesus has infiltrated the Muslim world in an unprecedented way. Muslims across the Middle East have lined up and sold out theaters in order to see a movie about Jesus and His sacrifice.

It's hard to deny that God is up to something in all this.

THE **PASSION**

"[The R rating is] appropriate. I don't think kids under thirteen should see it. BUT THE BIBLE IS R-RATED. There's always something in there that's shocking." —Mel Gibson

In July of 2004, *The Passion of the Christ* had surpassed $370 million in domestic box office revenue alone, earning the number eight spot on the all-time box office list behind *Titanic* and two *Star Wars* movies. Ultimately, the film is a passionate, beautiful, intense, and excruciating tribute to Jesus, and one thing is absolutely certain: Whoever sees this movie will walk away from the theater having seen something special. "I'm not a preacher and I'm not a pastor," Gibson said. "But I really feel my career was leading me to make this. The Holy Ghost was working through me on this film, and I was just directing traffic. I hope the film has the power to evangelize."

Notes

1. "Mel Gibson's 'Passion' Reclaims Top Box-Office Spot Over Easter Weekend," Associated Press, *http://apnews.myway.com/article/20040411/D81SRCK01.html* (accessed July 26, 2004).

2. Gene Edward Veith, "Stirring up Passions," *World*, March 13, 2004, p. 25.

3. Pamela McClintock, "'Passion' clashin' fills Rooney's mailbag," *Variety*, *www.variety.com/index. asp?layout=upsell_article&articleID=VR1117901662&categoryID=14&cs=1* (accessed April 9, 2004).

4. Michael Medved, "The Passion and Prejudice," *Christianity Today*, March 2004, p. 38.

5. Ibid, p. 40.

6. Jane Johnson Struck, "Mel's Passion," *Today's Christian Woman*, March 2004, p. 39.

7. Phil Boatwright, "Mel Gibson: 'The Passion' will 'bring people closer together,'" February 19, 2004, *www.bpnews.net/bpnews.asp?ID=17680* (accessed April 9, 2004).

8. Holly McClure, "Mel Gibson's Passion," *www.crosswalk.com/fun/movies/1195712.html* (accessed August 26, 2003).

9. Gayle MacDonald, "Christ Complex," *The Globe and Mail*, December 21, 2002, p. R1.

10. Ibid.

11. Ibid.

12. Holly McClure, "Mel Gibson's Passion," *www.crosswalk.com/fun/movies/1195712.html* (accessed August 26, 2003).

13. Gayle MacDonald, "Christ Complex," *The Globe and Mail*, December 21, 2002, p. R1.

14. Jack Valenti quoted at *www.newsmax.com. www.newsmax.com/cgi-bin/showinside. pl?a=2003/7/22/223018* (accessed July 26, 2004).

15. Holly McClure, "Mel Gibson's Passion," *www.crosswalk.com/fun/movies/1195712.html* (accessed August 26, 2003).

16. Mel Gibson quoted at HollywoodJesus.com. *www.hollywoodjesus.com/passion_review2.htm* (accessed July 26, 2004).

17. Holly McClure, "Gibson's Passion for Jesus," *www.arentstv.org* (accessed August 26, 2003).

18. Holly McClure, "Mel Gibson's Passion," *www.crosswalk.com/fun/movies/1195712.html* (accessed August 26, 2003).

19. Peter J. Boyer, *The New Yorker*, September 2003.

20. "Mel Is Still as Faithful as Ever," Associated Press, August 15, 2002.

21. Mel Gibson interviewed by Bill O'Reilly, Fox News (January 15, 2004).

22. (reported in the book *Jesus at the Movies*, page 163).

23. "Inside the Vatican," Zenit News Agency, Urbi et Orbi Communications, New Hope, KY: March 2003.

24. "ADL Statement on Mel Gibson's 'The Passion," *www.adl.org/PresRele/Mise_00/4275_00.asp* (accessed August 2003).

25. Associated Press, "Mel Gibson's 'Passion' Makes Waves," August 8, 2003, online at CBSNews. com. *www.cbsnews.com/stories/2003/08/08/entertainment/main567445.shtml* (accessed July 26, 2004).

26. "ADL Statement on Mel Gibson's 'The Passion," *www.adl.org/PresRele/Mise_00/4275_00.asp* (accessed August 2003).

27. Ibid.

28. Michael Medved, "The Passion and Prejudice," *Christianity Today*, March 2004, p. 38.

29. Associated Press, "Mel Gibson's Controversial 'Passion,'" August 12, 2003 online at WNDU. *www.wndu.com/entertainment/082003/entertainment_21284.php* (accessed on July 26, 2004).

30. Nacha Cattan, "ADL Interfaith Official Quits, Stance on Film Questioned," November 14, 2003, *www.forward.com/issues/2003/03.11.14/news7.korn.html* (accessed December 20, 2003).

31. Michael Medved, "The Passion and Prejudice," *Christianity Today*, March 2004, p. 40.

32. "Gibson's Film 'Passion' Inflames Tempers," CNN, August 14, 2003.

33. Lorena Munoz, Larry B. Stammer, "Fallout Over 'Passion' Deepens," *Los Angeles Times*, January 23, 2004, p. E1.

34. Ibid.

35. Tim Rutten, "Passions Are Swirling Anew," *Los Angeles Times*, January 21, 2004, Regarding Media, p. E1.

36. "Bahrain bans Gibson's 'The Passion of the Christ,'"Yahoo News, April 1, 2004.

37. Nadia Abou El-Magd, "Gibson's 'Passion' a Hit Among Arabs," Associated Press, April 5, 2004.

PRODUCER

X-Men 3 — 2006
Fantastic Four — 2005
In My Sleep — 2003
Hangman's Curse — 2003
Blizzard — 2003
X-Men 2 — 2003
Shoot or Be Shot — 2002
Planet of the Apes — 2001

Left Behind — 2000
X-Men — 2000
Opie Gone Mad — 1999
Inspector Gadget — 1999
Mighty Joe Young — 1998
The Spitting Image — 1997
High Incident (TV) — 1996
Hackers — 1995
The Puppet Masters — 1994

Hocus Pocus — 1993
Captain Ron — 1992
Star Trek VI — 1991
Plymouth (TV) — 1991
The Perfect Weapon — 1991
Flight of the Intruder — 1991
Star Trek V: The Final Frontier — 1989
Star Trek IV — 1986
Star Trek III — 1984

DIRECTOR

High Incident (TV) — 1996

MAKING THE
BLOCKBUSTER

02 RALPH WINTER

⊠ MAKING THE BLOCKBUSTER

"It's fun to make all the plates spin—from finding the property to finding the team, the financing, the director, the writers, putting it all together, getting it to an audience, marketing it, and distributing it. All those things are a lot of fun and energizing, and seeing the end result play successfully in front of an audience is really fun." —Ralph Winter

Outside Hollywood, the job of the producer is a bit of a mystery. Many people ask, "What exactly does a producer do?" The answer is never very short—perhaps because producers do so much; in truth, a producer is often the single consistent force that ensures that a movie is made.

True producers, in actuality, are involved in nearly every aspect of a film's preproduction, postproduction, and on-set production. Producers do everything from finding and optioning or buying a script, to attaching a cast, to helping the director find and choose locations. The producer brings everyone together and makes sure a film stays on budget, has enough money, and achieves its production and distribution goals.

One of the most prolific, consistently successful, and well-respected producers in Hollywood is Ralph Winter.

In an interview with radio commentator Dick Staub, Winter commented on the role of the producer in Hollywood movies. "In the feature film business, the person who gets to get up and gets the award for Best Picture is the producer," Winter said. "So, in feature films, that is the highest level. The producer is really the champion. They're the one that holds the flag up from the very beginning to get the material, get the financing, all the way from acquiring and finding the story, recognizing it, delivering it, and now through all the venues from home video and merchandising and licensing. A lot of my job is waving pom poms and keeping the team going and inspiring them to do their job."[1]

Whether you prefer action movies, science fiction epics, comedies, family movies, comic book stories, or Christian films like *Left Behind*, chances are Ralph Winter has made a movie for you. From science fiction epics like *Star Trek* and *Planet of the Apes* to low-budget films like *Hangman's Curse*, Winter's expertise truly spans every size and genre of films. And as one of the most influential Christians making movies today, Winter truly enjoys his job.

"The best part of the job is really the opening night screenings, watching an audience react and enjoy the movie the way you designed it," Winter said. "This kind of work involves a lot of travel, so I've been able to travel all over the world. It's a fun deal, making little movies, half a million, $2 million movies, as well as making $120 million dollar movies."

In terms of helping to educate and network with Christian filmmakers, Winter is deeply involved in a number of groundbreaking circles. He lends his time as a judge for the spiritually focused Damah Film Festival, as a staff member at Act One: Writing for Hollywood (a Christian screenwriting school), as a regular speaker at Christian entertainment conferences, universities, and seminaries, and as a friend to numerous ministries, including The Veracity Project.

He also doles out wisdom in large doses for those ambitious Christian filmmakers who hope to tell stories on the giant screen. Whether he's speaking to a large crowd of people, lecturing in a classroom, or on the phone one-on-one, Winter gives it to you straight.

"What is always going to make a way in Hollywood is talent," Winter said. "There's lots of people that have high ideals, but do you have the talent? Can you tell a story, can you direct, can you do makeup, can you do whatever field it is you want to do? And can you do that at a level that gets attention?"

Winter himself has spent years perfecting the art of producing, and he's gotten a lot of attention along the way.

A CALL TO **HOLLYWOOD**

"I want people to be inspired by stories of how we as humans are figuring out the journey of life, how to make it all work. What are the resources, what are the pitfalls? HOW DO PEOPLE MAKE IT, HOW DO WE LIVE TOGETHER, HOW DO WE GET ALONG? I think that our faith can inform how those stories are told so that ultimately, what I hope we're doing is stirring up cravings inside of people, about what life is about." —Ralph Winter

Winter never intended to be a filmmaker. After graduating from UC Berkeley as a history major, he fell into a job where he made videos for a chain of Broadway department stores. The chain had approximately fifty stores in five states comprised of more than five thousand employees, and they used training videos to standardize their processes. It was there that Winter was first introduced the medium of film and video on the creative filmmaking side, and in the midst of the job, he discovered that he had a knack for it.

But it didn't happen right away. In the three and a half years Winter worked for Broadway, he said that he made some videos that were downright terrible—so bad, in fact, that he burned them. Over time, he improved his craft and learned how to tell a story in the midst of making short industrial films about employee benefits, how to greet customers, or how to take inventory.

"I made about fifty industrial training, customer service videos for the stores, and I learned a lot about filmmaking and telling stories and having fun," Winter said. "Once I got in at the Broadway and started to gain those skills, I started to make little short programs for the church, for the kids Vacation Bible School or the mission trip to Mexico, or the Stewardship campaign, or the vision and purpose of why the church needs to change the goals statement."

Throughout his life, Winter has been deeply involved in the Church. He acted in a number of church plays and musicals, including *Godspell*, in which he played John the Baptist, and a *Narnia* presentation that saw him playing the part of Aslan. His deep booming voice is naturally suited to theater, and he confirmed that the thrill of acting was always the audience reaction, something that carried over to his work in Hollywood.

Even when he began making videos and short films for the Church, Winter said it was inspiring to create something that affected the life of the Church body. Now that Winter is a well-established Hollywood powerhouse, one might think he'd have less time to get involved with church life, but this is not the case. These days, Winter leads his own small group to discuss film issues at Glendale Presbyterian Church, where he has been a member for years.

"What we do is take the Academy Award best picture nominees and each week go through and say, 'Okay, what's the story about? Who's the hero? How does what that story is about match up with who we are as Christians?'" Winter said in one interview. He elaborated on the kinds of questions he asks in his film discussion group. "And now open your Bible—how do we make sense of this? Why does the Academy honor this film, and should we honor it as well? And if so, what can we learn from it?"[2]

Winter also spent a good amount of time working with his youth group when he was younger and even considered going into full-time ministry after graduation. It was at that point when he reached a crossroads in his life.

"I was either going to go to seminary or teach or go to graduate school, and I fell into this stuff at the Broadway Department stores," Winter said. "From there, I got an opportunity to move into Paramount, and I worked in postproduction for a few years on their film shows, delivering those to the network."

When he joined Paramount, a job he would keep for another three and half years, Winter helped the company complete postproduction duties on a variety of TV shows for various networks, including *Happy Days*, *Laverne & Shirley*, *Mork & Mindy*, and *Taxi*, among others.

And after his years of cranking out industrial training videos and learning the nuances of the more industrial side of filmmaking, the exposure to the high-level studio version of TV production captivated Winter immediately. "Being exposed to a higher skill level, I really got the bug and figured out that I wasn't going to go to seminary," Winter said. "This was something I felt God calling in my life—that I still can be serving God by doing this."

Like others profiled in this book, Winter struggled with the idea that he could work in the movies while serving God at the same time. Many artists and filmmakers pursuing this career have to work through this idea one way or another. The irony is that Christians ought to feel exhilarated by entering into the most influential industry in the world, not inhibited. It is distinctly possible that in Hollywood, Christians have more opportunities to reach people for Christ than almost any other mission field. And thankfully, it appears as though the common tendency to feel bad for wanting to make movies is shifting in the opposite direction.

While working in postproduction at Paramount, Winter met and got to know a number of filmmakers, directors, and others—relationships that eventually helped land him his first big movie job as an associate producer on *Star Trek 3*.

"[When I] moved out to be an associate producer on *Star Trek 3*, having worked closely with them on *Star Trek 2*, I was sort of off and running," Winter said.

After making *Star Trek 3*, Winter continued to get to know the industry—but it didn't take long; in a very short amount of time, his resumé morphed into a very long rap sheet of big time Hollywood movies.

But because he has made Hollywood his career and mission field, Winter hasn't made it through unscathed. Along the way, he has taken flack from other Christians who have criticized him just for working in Hollywood, an industry dismissed as impure by some in the Church. "[Some Christians] think if you're not making movies about Jesus or the end times, what good are you?" Winter said.

Even though Winter has even helped produce several Christian movies—even one that deals with end times—he still gets criticism from time to time.

"People were coming up to me and asking, 'How can you say you're a Christian but make a movie like *X-Men* or *Planet of the Apes*, which implies evolution?'" Winter told one interviewer. "And with the movie

Hocus Pocus, people were saying, 'How can you call yourself a Christian, but make a movie about three witches and a talking cat?' But, what I tell them is to look at the movie ... look at how the young man in the movie was willing to lay down his life to save another, and look at how at the end, evil—the witches were destroyed. Are these not Christian principles? I have absolutely zero patience for that stuff."[3]

Tolerating Christians should be the least of Winter's worries in an industry fraught with cutthroat competition and films featuring more gratuitous sex and violence than ever. Some would say this is why Christians shouldn't work in Hollywood, but Winter's influence on one scene in the massive Hollywood blockbuster film *X-Men* is well-known to many.

In discussing the film with *X-Men* director Brian Singer, Winter objected to a scene in which Magneto, the arch villain of the film, was supposed to kill a policeman.

"I had an adverse reaction to Magneto killing a cop in the scene at the train station," Winter said. "I spoke to the director, and he found a creative way to have Magneto fire the gun but have the bullet stop just short of hitting the police officer."[4]

As a result, that scene became one of the standouts in terms of character complexity and helped to shade the relationship between the film's arch-enemies, Magneto and Doctor Xavier—not to mention the fact that the special effect thrilled audiences and critics alike, becoming a well-loved scene.

One component of the script that drew Winter to the *X-Men* project as a whole was the overall theme of tolerance that runs throughout. "I got involved because of the script," Winter told one interviewer. "The issues, the ideas about tolerance and how we're gonna get along—I think those are timeless issues for our culture, and that's what attracted me. I've got experience doing big science fiction movies with large casts and lots of visual effects, but I think the ideas about tolerance are the things that attracted me to this franchise."[5]

The first *X-Men* film was littered with debate about how people should treat mutants (humans with extraordinary powers, such as being able to walk through walls or control the weather). In the midst of this debate about tolerance (and intolerance), the film pitted the mutant X-Men, the good guys, against a mutant criminal mastermind named Magneto, who had experienced persecution during the Holocaust as a child. His experience seeing his parents separated and presumably killed led him to mistrusting humans and especially their intolerance of mutants. Such a deep theme in a comic movie is rare indeed, but it acts as an example of Winter's standards for choosing projects.

In another overly simplified debate, many of the same Christians who have criticized Winter object to the whole idea of Christians seeing R-rated films in the first place. But Winter has polished up his reply for that objection. On the phone, Winter took no time to slam dunk the argument by saying, "Isn't it interesting for people that talk about that, and now *The Passion* has become the most successful R-rated movie of all time?

"Those people need to get over it," he continued. "I think it's old and tired. Read Brian Godawa's book *Hollywood Worldviews*. The appendix is worth the price of the book. Then don't read the Old Testament if you don't want to watch R-rated movies."

When talking to another interviewer, Winter echoed the sentiment, but employed another classic reply. "I always ask this one question: Did Jesus surround himself with R-rated people or not?"[6]

You would think that would shut up the majority of his critics.

In the meantime, Winter will continue to do what he does best. His mission field as a follower of Christ is Hollywood. And he has some very specific ideas about what Christians need to do to impact people's lives and change culture through the medium of film.

"Don't write stuff and produce stuff about answers—don't do that,"

Winter said. "Write stuff and produce stuff that will stir up cravings inside of us, because that's the DNA that God's put inside of us. You stir that stuff up, and that's where [people] want to go to church. That's when they want to talk about the good news. That's when they want to find out, *How do you get through this? How do you do this?* And when we stir up those cravings, we can point them to the other resources, and we can share that good news with them."

WHAT DOES **THE AUDIENCE** REALLY WANT TO SEE?

"Now there's always going to be people that are out there that are making material that exclusively is for a Christian audience. AND THAT'S NOT BAD, THAT'S JUST WHAT THEY'RE GOING AFTER. But I don't know that that's necessarily what other Christians that I hang out with in Hollywood want to make." —Ralph Winter

When Ralph Winter was brought on as a producer for a project called *Left Behind* being produced by Namesake Entertainment, he knew there was an audience primed to go to the theaters. The *Left Behind* book series was already a perennial best seller—a sure way of unlocking a word-of-mouth buzz for any movie. But after working on the project for only a short time, Winter left to go make *X-Men*, and the *Left Behind* project moved ahead, trying to make the most of its less than 4 million dollar budget.

But if *Left Behind* had been made for 100 million dollars, with a substantial marketing budget, some credible action stars, and some great special effects, people would be talking up the quality of the final product. To make a successful picture, a filmmaker has to know what the audience wants to see.

"That was really why I got involved with *Left Behind* at the beginning, was to help figure out how do we make [*Left Behind*] mainstream,"

Winter said. "That's why I helped select that director for that movie, Vic Sarin, because he's not a Christian. He's on the path, searching, looking. What could be better than having a guy as the director of the movie searching for the same things that Buck is looking for in *Left Behind*, as opposed to applying familiar answers to questions no one seems to be asking? The trick is to be in touch and to be commercial. What does the audience really want to see, and how do we connect with them? That's what studios are looking for all the time in the way they develop and distribute product."

Winter cites *The Passion of the Christ* as an example of how the studios try to serve their customers in the same way any other company would look to provide top quality customer service. In effect, the studios are in the business of supplying demands.

"I think [*The Passion*] opened up the audience," Winter said. "I think the studios are looking for, 'Okay, how can we get some of that audience to come back to the theaters again? What kind of product are they looking for?' So the studios are active in looking for that. But it's a mistake to think that Hollywood is going to want more Bible stories. They know there's a market, but I think Christians want good entertainment as much as the next person. [Christians] want stars and compelling entertainment."

Unfortunately, when Christian film critics point out that Hollywood needs to make more values-driven movies, they miss the fact that Hollywood is in the business of serving up good stories, not good messages. And these good stories must appeal to culture as a whole. While the studios want to make movies that will be attractive to a Christian audience seeking cleaner films, they also want to make movies that will be attractive to as many people as potentially possible. And real people are attracted to real stories about real life.

Life is filled with R-rated things, and sometimes the use of harsher material serves a very valuable purpose in terms of story. See examples in amazing films like *Schindler's List*, *Saving Private Ryan*, *To End All Wars*, *The Passion of the Christ*, *Magnolia*, and *The Big Kahuna*. But is this what audiences really want to see?

The key is the project, Winter said.

"Find a piece of material that the audience wants to see," Winter said. "It's about material, it's not just about execution, but it starts with material, and then it's how you execute that. I personally want to see, in this area, more Christians that want to make films that want to pursue it and have integrity. I'm tired of bumping into people who say they're Christians and don't treat people with respect or pay them a fair wage. Deal honestly. I think we're held accountable for that stuff. Unfortunately, those are the people that get some attention in Hollywood, and those are the people that smear the reputation of others that try to go at it with some integrity. I think integrity has to go along with excellence and the commerciality of what we're doing. Gotta have all three."

EXTENDING **INFLUENCE**

"Unfortunately, there's a perception that people want stuff handed to them, you know. Well, just give me this opportunity and I'll demonstrate that I'm the person. Just let me produce *Fantastic Four* or just let me produce *X-Men 9*, and I'll show you that I'm the person that can do it. THAT'S NOT WHERE I STARTED; that's not where they should start." —Ralph Winter

In the world of moviemaking magic, two Christian circles run a parallel track. One circle is an informal network of Christians who have worked and do work in Hollywood, making movies that reach massive audiences and working side-by-side with non-Christians to make an impact on that mission field. The second circle is called the Christian film industry, a grouping of lower budget production companies that make movies for a small segment of the Christian population who often buy their movies from Christian bookstores.

Both circles have an interest in changing culture through film. Both circles are accomplishing that in a different way. Ralph Winter has chosen the path of the former circle and has been very successful both in affecting masses of people with the stories he's involved in telling and in impacting the young Christians filmmakers he's helped along the way. No disrespect to the latter circle though—"[The Christian film industry] will still make movies, and they will still do well," Winter said. "I think there's people that will always buy that niche market material, you know, always. I'm interested in doing more mainstream stuff."

It's not surprising then that he has a wealth of advice for those looking to make their way and extend their influence in Hollywood. After twenty-plus years in the industry, Winter has met his share of filmmakers with ambitious Hollywood aspirations, but for such a gracious guy, he doesn't pretend it's easy to get ahead in the most competitive industry in the world. People have also tried to use his faith as common ground to pitch him story ideas, but Winter said he isn't a script reader. Those who want to chart a path in Hollywood have to dive in headfirst.

"You've got to get out there and do it," Winter said. "Find the material, find the resources to get it made, the filmmaking resources, and see what happens. And the filmmaking tools are out there; they're not expensive."

Just in case you missed it, Winter is challenging the next Richard Linklater-esque, low-budget, guerilla filmmaker to step into their passion and make a movie. Winter speaks from experience, extending his influence both in the Christian and mainstream marketplaces.

Case in point: his most recent independent film project with famed Christian writer Frank Peretti titled *Hangman's Curse*. Winter tackled the project with Peretti because of the author's crossover appeal to the mainstream audience. Peretti's books have caught on in both the Christian and mainstream markets, and yet, his movie was still a hard sell due to its limited resources. In looking to extend his influence in both the Christian and secular market, Winter helped get *Hangman's Curse* off the ground and even hopes to later release a whole line of Peretti movies.

So what can replace a multi-million dollar marketing budget? Two things: ingenuity and tenacity.

The film released in September 2003, rode out its tenure in the theaters for eight weeks in the six biggest box office markets, cities like Los Angeles and New York, and slammed onto DVD in late March 2004, selling quickly in both the Christian market and in general market locations like Costco, Wal-Mart, Best Buy, and Target. Anybody can market a film with a multi-million dollar budget and make the world aware of its existence, but getting people to buy the DVD or shell out eight to ten bucks for a movie ticket is another game altogether. When all is said and done, *Hangman's Curse* will make its money back because of an immense amount of underground buzz building ... and just plain sweat.

To extend influence in Hollywood, especially with a Christian film, it takes an amazing amount of persistence. "It's hard work to do grassroots marketing like on *Hangman's Curse*," Winter said. "We didn't do any TV ads. But we did hundreds of radio interviews. Frank Peretti [traveled] on a bus through six major markets, shaking hands, signing autographs, talking to audiences, screening the film. It's hard work. There's no easy way about it. It's calling up people on the phone and convincing them that, you know, this is a good movie and they oughta want to see it."

And this is where Ralph Winter excels as a producer, though he's adept at making and promoting the $100 million movies, too. He can get down and dirty and work hard, and he respects those who worked hard to get where they're at as well. Does that mean that Christians who want to make movies should simply steamroll their way into writing their screenplay or making their long awaited feature film? Do Christians need to get to work?

Well, yes. But that statement should be qualified. There are any number of screenwriters and directors in Southern California and around the world. What separates the wheat from the chaff, in Winter's experience anyway, is a lack of research, desire, and doing quality work.

And here it is, the biggest lesson a filmmaker can get from a Hollywood producer, the man who can read their script or watch their demo reel and decide whether or not to make a movie with them—"Professionally, I think it's about doing the work," Winter said. "There are thousands and thousands of screenwriters in town that are mediocre—they don't kind of want to hear that, but they are. You can't fault them for trying—I think it's great—[but] there are plenty of things to learn from. It's surprising to me how many don't take the basic steps and just do some homework. There's plenty of stuff out there and screenwriting classes, not to mention all the Academy and Writers Guild Award-winning screenplays that can be studied. There's no easy way around it; it's not gonna fall in your lap. It didn't fall in my lap."

And not only do aspiring filmmakers have to do the work, but they have to make friends along the way. Winter landed his first producing job as an associate producer on *Star Trek 3* because he had worked with the team on *Star Trek 2* and impressed them enough to inquire after his services on their next project. But how do you build up enough contacts to land a job like that?

It's simple. The studios are always hiring for something, whether it's in production, postproduction, home video, maintenance, or accounting. Aspiring filmmakers should get in and get some experience, see if they really want to work in the movies after all—not to mention the fact that there are film and video production companies of some sort in just about every urban center around the country. And now the Church is latching onto these kinds of tools as well, producing short segments to give their announcements or to show what happened on a recent missions trip. What better way for would-be filmmakers to polish up their production skills than by helping their local church produce their announcements or recent missions trip documentary on video?

"Get a job on the lot, any job as an assistant, something so that you get exposed to what that all is," Winter advised. "Every kid from the Midwest can't work at Fox, but there's also tremendous opportunities out there in terms of commercials and industrials, public access, universities."

Networking seems to be a big issue in Christian filmmaking circles. The truth is that networking is vital to working in Hollywood, no matter who you are. You have get to know a lot of people before you start to find out who is talented, who works hard, and who you can turn to in an emergency.

Many Christians tend to wear blinders when it comes to the networking issue, trying to network primarily with other Christians, while some think that because they themselves are Christians, other Hollywood believers will hire them on the spot. Again, it comes back to being good at what you do, whether it's acting, writing, directing, or producing.

In fact, in many ways, beliefs should be less of an issue when selecting who to work with on a film. Winter, who has a history in helping other talented Christians get their movies made, said networking is fine, to a point.

"People who have talent and similar desires should network and find ways of helping each other," he said. "I don't know if there necessarily needs to be some underground Christian network movement. I like the idea of different pockets of resistance that are attenuated to different needs and desires. There are some Christians in Hollywood that are talented at [making] horror movies. Only a few would actually be able to stomach that, but the ones who do, they know who to network with to make those thrillers."

THE PRODUCER'S TIP BOOK: **A SUMMARY**

"I like making movies. I WANT TO MAKE A LOT OF MOVIES."
—Ralph Winter

Christians filmmakers, take this lesson to heart: Talent and hard work can't be replaced by who you know. In fact, hard work and talent supercede who you know. Research your field, your craft, or your desired profession; discover all there is to know about it; and then do it until you can do it right. Once you've done what you believe is your very best, then networking can be a valuable tool in getting the product of your hard work noticed.

Next, keep your mind on the commerciality of the movie you're working on. If you want big studios to put up big money for your script or to hire you for their next movie, look for high concept scripts or projects that people will actually want to see. How do you gauge the audience? Read the Hollywood bibles to keep current with industry trends (*Daily Variety*, *The Hollywood Reporter*), watch the box office charts every week, and get a subscription to a film magazine or two. Much of this information is also available online.

Future producers beware: Your job is not to be a director's nightmare, but a director's cheerleader. On the set, in postproduction, or when meeting your director for the first time, make him or her understand that your job is to support him or her in any way possible, although you still have to keep a close eye on the budget, whether it's $50, $500,000, or $5 million, but positive reinforcement works wonders.

A note on *The Passion of the Christ*: Winter believes Mel Gibson caught lightning in a bottle with *The Passion of the Christ*. "I think Mel made a movie out of his own enthusiasm and interest in that topic, and I don't think he made it as a Christian film; he made it as, it's a love poem," Winter said. "It's something that he wanted to do and figured that if he could rally some support behind it, he would. I don't think you're going to be able to duplicate that again. Mel is a Hollywood star, but he did it outside of the system; he funded it with his own money."

Another surprising factoid from the producer's tip book: There is a shortage of good ideas in Hollywood. Have you ever wondered why you see twenty bad movie sequels hit theaters every year? The reason is that good, well-structured script ideas are very rare. What does this mean for those who think they have a good idea? If your idea is truly a good one, then you're already a step ahead of a majority of those in your position.

Finally, a bit of advice for anyone with artistic aspirations: Did you know that church could be your very own film school and training ground? Many churches these days actually have production material on hand to tape services, record events, or shoot commercials for announcements. Plug into your local church or find the church in your area that can serve as your training ground. Bonus: While you're learning to fiddle around with a camera, you can serve the kingdom at the same time!

Notes

1. Dick Staub interview online at: *www.dickstaub.com/culturewatch.php?record_id=612* (accessed June 21, 2004).
2. Ibid.
3. L. Pat Williams, "Winter Storm," RELEVANT magazine, March/April 2004, p. 39.
4. Teresa Blythe, "Hollywood: Faith on the Set," *Presbyterians Today*, May 2003.
5. Ibid.
6. L. Pat Williams, "Winter Storm," RELEVANT magazine, March/April 2004, p. 39.

HOLLYWOOD project
FILMOGRAPHY

DIRECTOR

Around the World in 80 Days — 2004
Secondhand Lions — 2003
Smallville (TV) — 2001
The Iron Giant — 1999
Dennis the Menace Strikes Again — 1998
Dancer, Texas Pop. 81 — 1998
North Shore — 1987

WRITER

Secondhand Lions — 2003
Dancer, Texas Pop. 81 — 1998

PRODUCER

North Shore — 1987

HOLLYWOOD project
FILMOGRAPHY

03 TIM McCANLIES

⊠ SEARCHING FOR UNIVERSAL TRUTH

> "I went to graduate film school and finally ran out of film courses to take. So I came out to L.A. with everything I owned in an $800 van. I went right to Hollywood, thinking that's where the center of the film business would be, thinking that all the studios must be right there. I was so naïve; I had no idea if screenwriters really made good money or not." —Tim McCanlies

The films of Tim McCanlies capture a variety of bold styles—from surf movie to animation adventure, college comedy to stark drama—while driving home a small range of themes with uncanny similarity. His movies are a collection of choreographed digressions into the questions of adolescence, growing up, leaving innocence, discovering the complexities of manhood, and the myriad of emotions involved therein. Peruse the aisle that features McCanlies' films, and you'll come across the youthful ambitions of the cult classic surf movie North Shore, the post-high school whimsy of *Dancer, Texas, Pop. 81*, and the popular children's movie, *The Iron Giant*, which draws on the Christ-figure metaphor.

These films and others display the McCanlies trademark depth, tenderness, and charm, and his characters always experience a kind of breakthrough, often involving boys who are clawing their way into manhood. In this sense, his films are surely passionate and even spiritual, due to their emotional depth, intense metaphors, and explorations of simple but powerful truths.

These issues are important to a discussion of excellence in spiritual film in several ways. First, this discussion will explore the idea that spiritual truths, or God's truths, whether spoken by believer or nonbeliever, are still truths. Second, it is important to discover the unique quality that draws emotion and depth out of a story in a way that has eluded most Christian filmmakers. Filmmakers seeking excellence must heed the lessons buried in films like these as they continue to pursue Hollywood's holy grail: the making of a monetarily successful and powerful feature film with a truly compelling storyline.

To get an understanding of why Tim McCanlies always manages to make consistently powerful and deeply emotional movies will require an extended look at his film *Secondhand Lions*.

SECONDHAND LIONS

"THAT'S THE MAGICAL THING ABOUT MOVIES, you know—suddenly you can just be Indiana Jones or a kid without a father and not much of a mother being dumped off with these two crazy guys. I think it makes us feel like we're all part of the human race sometimes."
—Tim McCanlies

McCanlies finished and released his second movie as a director in late 2003. The movie, titled *Secondhand Lions*, stars Robert Duvall, Michael Caine, and Haley Joel Osment. McCanlies talked about *Secondhand Lions* with enthusiasm, as the film was gearing up to hit theaters across the country.

When discussing the genesis of the powerful little movie, McCanlies said his idea sparked into story when he decided to write about two curmudgeonly old men, later named Hub and Garth. "It started with Hub and Garth. I mean, I love sort of larger-than-life Texas men," he said. "I started with these two characters and thought, *What if I brought a kid into that situation? What would that do?*"

As his ideas continued to develop, McCanlies stumbled across a documentary that served as inspiration for one of the film's most powerful themes.

"[The documentary] was about men in prison and how 99 or 100 percent have no father or an abusive father," McCanlies said. "It was just this startling statistic on how these kids were messed up. And it seemed like something that nobody was even talking about or wondering about. I mean, what it is that men teach boys? It's as if there's something in boys that's untamable and wild that needs to be civilized, and that men do that for boys. I was wondering about that, and it sort of coalesced into that speech that Hub gives young men [in the movie]."

In the film, a boy named Walter (Osment) embodies this theme when his reckless and greedy mother drops him off at the ranch of his loosely related uncles. When his mother leaves in a rush, two things become clear: He's there to stay for the summer; and she isn't interested in mothering—only in discovering the fortune the uncles are rumored to have stashed.

The film seems sentimental from the outset, but approaches its subject with humor and fun. The film attacks the theme of fatherhood and the father figure with measured punches, as Walter starts to see in his uncles something he's been missing all his life. When Hub (Duvall) teaches a few older boys a lesson, Walter overhears him giving the boys a speech about what it means to be a man. Garth notices Walter's interest and informs him that Hub is giving the boys his "becoming a man" speech. It is at this point that Walter adopts a quest, a thematic journey that had been foreshadowed. Walter wants to discover the key to becoming a man, and he believes that his uncles hold the key to this particular mystery.

When Walter demands to hear Hub's speech, Hub gives him a portion of the speech to soothe his earnest youth. Again, Osment plays the part of innocence well, although his cracking voice hints at impending puberty. Walter wants so badly to live up to something, to live up to someone and their ideals. He's grappling for a standard to tell him what's right, and it's a painfully clear picture of our society's need for fathers.

McCanlies' intent in making the movie comes across when Hub finally dispenses with his passionate wisdom, saying to young Walter, "Sometimes the things that may or may not be true are the things that a man needs to believe in the most: that people are basically good; that honor, courage, and virtue mean everything; that power and money, money and power mean nothing; that good always triumphs over evil; and I want you to remember this: that love … true love … never dies. You remember that, boy. You remember that. Doesn't matter if it's true or not. You see, a man should believe in those things, because those are the things worth believing in."

As Hub winds down this portion of the speech, Walter, through tears and crackling voice, asks him for the rest of it, saying, "I can't be a good man until you give me the rest of the speech, right?" Not only does this scene make for fantastic cinema, but it also brings the story and its message to the fore without slighting either one.

Even Focus on the Family's famously rigid *Plugged In* magazine gave high marks to *Secondhand Lions*. An article on the film by Bob Smit-houser praised the film for its messages about befriending the elderly and urging senior citizens to finish strong in life.[1]

The key component that separates most Christian films from *Secondhand Lions* can be summed up in one word: story. Every filmmaker in the film industry today talks about the importance of story, but do they really mean it? McCanlies might have written a movie that followed one of any number of fatherless prisoners talking desperately about how much he needed a father when he was younger, quoting the statistics through teary eyes. He might have played up the comic schtick; instead, Mc-Canlies chose to embed this particular idea into a storyline filled with rich subtext, characters, and adventure. After all, *Secondhand Lions* is not a movie about the fact that boys need fathers. The movie is about one boy who needs a father and gets two old Texas uncles instead. The story prevails, and thus, the theme comes across even more powerfully.

By the end of the film, we know that if it weren't for these two kindly old adventurers, Walter would have lost his innocence at a young age and ended up a statistic in a documentary. Ultimately, the theme of the movie reaches high, suggesting that people should believe in things others might tell them are too idealistic or unrealistic—like love, truth, and character. The movie is an inspiring triumph that presents a realistic portrait of a boy existing in an all too common situation, while achiev-ing uncommon results.

THE **HISTORY** OF McCANLIES

"I think I have a certain sensibility, a certain mix of comedy and drama, A CERTAIN SORT OF ODD WORLDVIEW THAT ONLY I CAN DO, and it's such a painful process." —Tim McCanlies

McCanlies is a longtime writer who, from his early grade-school days, found himself to be a lover of words with "a turn of phrase." His teachers encouraged him throughout his schooling to continue to pursue writing, and while other students worked on forming sentences around the word of the day, he would craft wildly original mobster stories or science fiction tales.

"It seemed like I was always that odd kid in the corner who could just write and do funny things," he shared. "I remember I used to read Tom Swift Jr. books, and I would try to write one, you know. I didn't know that it was supposed to be hard."

For McCanlies, who is inherently creative and a lover of Abbot and Costello, the jump to writing movies was an obvious one. He first attended Texas A&M University where he earned a bachelor's degree in drama. Later, when he determined that film was his primary passion, he enrolled in the graduate film program at the University of Texas. Once there, McCanlies said his appetite for education was insatiable, as he took every film class offered and watched as many movies as he could find.

"They had ten or twelve different film societies on campus that showed two or three movies a night," McCanlies said. "I got to see all of the Kurosawa films and stuff that you'd never get to see and probably still don't. You see your first Bergman film and you go, 'Wow, there's wholly other kinds of movies out there.'"

As the world opened up to the young writer and he exhausted the resources of the film program, the only logical step was westward. "Hollywood was this strange foreign country on the other side of the Rockies where anyone who had ever gone, had never returned," he said. McCanlies loaded up his van and moved to Hollywood.

Despite humble beginnings, which are often the starting point in stories like this one, it didn't take long for McCanlies to make his mark. After cutting his teeth in college, writing short films, plays, and a feature film script for his thesis, he landed an agent.

"[My thesis] actually got me some agents in Hollywood, not good agents, but agents nonetheless," he said. "But it was a good four or five years out here before I got signed by CAA [Creative Artists Agency]."

Here he came across the age-old screenwriting question: How many scripts do you have to write in order to get noticed by the Hollywood elite? Obviously it's not that simple, because even McCanlies admits that his first few screenplays were the typical, autobiographical stories that are common from young, inexperienced screenwriters.

"It was, I guess, my fourth script and my seventh script that got me noticed," McCanlies remembered. "I wrote [my fourth] script because I was a big jazz fan, and Harlem in the early '30s was a really interesting place, so I wrote sort of a Chandleresque mystery set in Harlem with a black lead. I said this is so far removed from who I am, if I can pull this off, then I really am a writer."

A few days after sending out the script, McCanlies got a call from the powerful and influential Creative Artists Agency. The agents at CAA noticed he didn't have an agent yet, wanted to talk to him, and signed him soon after.

Not long after landing his agent, McCanlies landed a writing and direct- ing deal at Disney, where he worked for several years. The Disney deal led very quickly to work on a film project with a former USC student who had done a surfing documentary.

"They had come up with this idea [for a film], but they didn't have a writer. So Disney said, 'Okay, well, here you go.' That day we got on a plane to Hawaii, and there I was, in the middle of writing a surfing movie. [I] didn't know anything about it, but had a month to write a script."

That film was *North Shore,* the cult classic surf movie that has inspired generations of surfers with its catchy slang, its depiction of surfing territorialism, and its story, that of an underdog surfer from Arizona learning how to surf in Hawaii, which has the best waves in the world. The movie showed the sport in a soulful and mystical light that created an underground sensation and still stands as one of surfing's greatest films, alongside *Big Wednesday* and *Endless Summer.* McCanlies chuckles when he realizes how he contributed to the legend behind surfing and the Hawaiian mythos in particular.

"I'd read somewhere that Eskimos have like three hundred words for snow, [so I thought] well, Hawaiians have like three hundred expressions for different kinds of surf," he said laughing. "And now everyone believes that as if it's true, because it's the North Shore."

After *North Shore,* McCanlies was still under contract with Disney, but he found himself increasingly frustrated with the studio and the movies they churned out. "[Disney was] making this thing called *The Rescue* at the time, which was like preteens with machine guns breaking their fathers out of North Korean prisons. And I said, 'Why the heck?'"

McCanlies felt bound in more ways than one. Disney's head of production at the time, Jeffery Katzenberg, who later became one of the three founders of Dreamworks, had instituted a "no dust" rule. Essentially, all the films that went into production were to have a thoroughly urban focus, ruling out films in rural settings. "They had all these sort of odd rules, and I said, 'Well, I don't agree with this rule.'"

"They sat me down and said, 'Okay, [one of] your three choices [is] one of the *Ernest* movies ...' Like *Ernest Goes to Camp,* where this guy is basically just this punching bag for ninety minutes. I had already screened one of those movies, and I [thought] it was morally reprehensible, so that was off the table. The other two ideas were a talking dog or an invisible kid goes to high school. And I said, 'Well, I don't want to write any of those.' And they said 'Tough, pick one.'"

Instead, McCanlies refused to write any of the three stories and threw a fit in the Disney commissary. His employers told him to take thirty days off, basically putting him out of commission to think about it. Never one to squander an opportunity, McCanlies turned their punishment on its head and used his time off to write.

"So I said, 'I'm going to write a script in this thirty days that breaks all of their rules. And I wrote *Dancer, Texas*, which was as dusty as I could possibly make it."

Dancer, Texas, also titled *Dancer, Texas, Pop. 81*, became McCanlies' directorial debut and a critical hit that found a modest audience on video. McCanlies assembled a small team to shoot the powerful little movie for under $2 million, hiring four very talented young actors to play the primary characters, including Peter Facinelli, Breckin Meyer, Ethan Embry, and Eddie Mills, all of whom have since gone on to film and TV careers.

"Most of the stuff they get offered is movies where teenagers have sex and then their heads get torn off," McCanlies said about tracking down his young cast. "To do something where they really got to show their chops, every young actor that was not a big name really wanted to do it because they actually got to be an actor. Every one of these guys wants to be Sean Penn; they're all so serious. Because we had no money, they all got scale, a couple thousand dollars a week on a four-week shooting schedule, twenty-four days. We were lucky to have so many terrific young actors wanting to do it. And they've all gone on to great stuff."

DEEPLY **SPIRITUAL**, NONRELIGIOUS

"I think the temptation would be to get a little sillier with [*Secondhand Lions*] and to go a little more comic, play the Grumpy Old Men sort of schtick. AND THAT'S NOT WHAT I WANT TO DO; I think people are really funny when they don't mean to be sometimes." —Tim McCanlies

There is a quality to all of McCanlies' films that is highly compelling and emotional. There is also one common thread: McCanlies' voice, the driving heart of his films, always pursues an aspect of humanity that is complex and spiritual, yet universal, as it dips below the surface.

In *North Shore*, a young surfer from Arizona who grew up surfing wave pools goes on a trip to Hawaii where he finds a mentor and learns the secrets to surfing the hottest surf spots in the world. Along the way, he makes some crazy friends, brushes with the locals, and becomes a man. The touching story is a reminder of McCanlies' own westerly journey of discovery, during which he also became a man.

The Iron Giant is the first animated film McCanlies wrote, and in it, audiences can find a surprisingly moving portrait of Jesus and His sacrifice buried in what would seem like an almost ludicrous plotline about an alien robot who comes to earth and befriends a young boy. It's a simple story that also happens to depict, along with the Christ figure's sacrifice, the Iron Giant's pseudo-resurrection. While the story is reminiscent of *E.T.* in its handling of an alien encounter and a young boy, the metaphor of the sacrificial lamb cements the emotional investment of the audience in a deeply moving way.

These kind of "McCanlies-isms" are apparent in all his work. Many of the moments of sudden impact within his films come from nowhere, because in a children's movie, you expect light action and lots of fun—you don't expect to feel the power of a scene. But it's a pleasant surprise. "Movies that move us, for some reason, people get uncomfortable with, and they go, 'Wow, it's a little emotional, isn't it?' Like that's a bad thing," McCanlies said. "To me, the best movies do move you. But to really legitimately move someone, it kind of sneaks up on them."

Secondhand Lions features several of these scenes in which the audience is roundly blindsided by raw emotional power. The scene in which Walter finally tells Hub how badly he needs to hear what it means to become a man deftly secures the audience's investment for the rest of the movie. In looking at scenes like these—in which a non-Christian filmmaker is tackling spiritual issues that are pertinent to all of us, in which we're learning a truth about our lives—it seems as if Christians can and should be tackling similar topics on film.

COMMON **GRACE** AND UNIVERSAL **TRUTH**

"There's so much of a consciousness of it now [that] there's more kids who choose [filmmaking] as a career. As opposed to I can be a doctor, a lawyer—I can be in the film business. TO ME IT WAS JUST THIS TOTAL BLIND LEAP OFF A CLIFF. Nothing else was even in my worldview." —Tim McCanlies

McCanlies' films all contain a measure of depth and emotion that is startling. Where does this come from? "I think I'm trying to find universal truths or things that connect all of us," he said. "And I think movies, and all literature, are the thing that kind of helps us communicate. We communicate in metaphors with each other, but we kind of communicate the human condition and who I am and who you are, and it makes us feel less alone—and to get to live through someone else's eyes in a way and kind of be in someone else's skin, you know? I think it makes us feel like we're all part of the same human race sometimes."

Could it be that certain filmmakers and their films afford deeper access to biblical truths than Christians and followers of Christ have been able to present in the pulpits and pews of our churches? Film, with its more intense quality, often offers a visceral thrill that sometimes feels like a whistling uppercut. Modern church doesn't often feel this way.

The question has two logical answers, both stemming from the concept of common grace, an idea that the world itself is not inherently evil and that God has blessed all of humankind and creation, including plants and animals. Common grace lends credence to the first answer, which is simply the notion that God can and will speak through whomever He needs to, revealing Himself to His people. God even spoke to Balaam through his own donkey in Numbers 22. If God can speak through a donkey's mouth, it's not that hard to imagine Him speaking through a non-Christian filmmaker.

Conversely, the second answer might be that the truths presented in the Bible are often adapted for literary purposes without the writer realizing the importance of the principles or themes he or she is utilizing. Filmmakers might even take biblical ideas out of context and use them for another purpose altogether. Truths presented in the Bible often find resonance in the hearts of people, Christian or otherwise.

In his book, *Reel Spirituality*, theologian Robert K. Johnston talks about a phenomenon in which nonbelievers recognize God's truth before believers do. In this discussion, he cites the story of Jonah as an example of this form of common grace.

"Here, it is the non-Israelite sailors who recognize God's possible involvement in their predicament long before Jonah does," Johnston said. "It is not the believer in Yahweh who acts in a godly way, but the pagan sailors. The irony is comical; the theology, crystal clear. God is involved with all of humankind and uses the wisdom and insight of nonbelievers to communicate his truth to people who believe."[2]

So whether God handpicks non-Christians and uses them to convey His messages to the world, or non-Christians simply identify with solid biblical truths, the fact is that God's truths are related to the world by the world. In other words, Christians do not have a monopoly on God's Word.

What can spiritual filmmakers take from such a statement? When they decide to make their movie, write about film, or discuss film with their friends, perhaps it's not too much to speak with humility on—even respect for—the Hollywood film industry, a virtual mission field with astounding influence in our culture.

For his part, McCanlies will keep on making movies. In an interview with a small Texas newspaper, McCanlies shared about his overall goals in making movies: "I'd like to do more challenging films, films where shots linger on faces, where you get to live in someone's skin."[3]

He echoes this comment on the phone from Hollywood: "There's a lot of movies that moved me, I guess, growing up. It's a fairly short list of really terrific films, and I'd just love to put one on that list."

As writers, filmmakers, teachers, critics, and astute watchers of film seeking to change hearts and legitimately move people, we share this goal with Tim McCanlies.

NOTES

1. Bob Smithouser, *Plugged In*, *www.pluggedinonline.com/movies/movies/a0001497.cfm* (accessed June 21, 2004).
2. Robert K. Johnston, *Reel Spirituality* (Baker Academic: 2001).
3. Cary L. Roberts, "Iron Writer," *Austin Chronicle*, August 9, 1999, *www.auschron.com/issues/vol18/issue49/screens.mccanlies.html* (accessed June 21, 2004).

PRODUCER

Cliché — 2003

Hometown Legend — 2002

DIRECTOR

Cliché — 2003

04 DALLAS JENKINS

⊠ THE CHRISTIAN FILM INDUSTRY

"There are some who believe that Christian bookstores shouldn't exist and that Christians should
work harder and that we should all be part of salt
and light. I happen to believe in Christian bookstores;
I believe there is a place for them. But at the same
time, I'm an artist, and I believe that you should be
able to make films the way you want to make them."
—Dallas Jenkins

In the months leading up to its release, the movie *Left Behind* generated
more buzz than any other Christian film project prior to that time. If
ever there was an audience primed for a massive theatrical release by
word of mouth buzz and incredible book sales, this was it.

When *Left Behind* debuted on video in outlets ranging from Costco
to Christian bookstores as a way to advertise for the film's upcoming
theatrical release, the video release essentially acted as the film's official

market bow, selling more than 3 million copies, while its subsequent theater take was more than disappointing.

Some people said the movie represented the best of what Christians could produce. Others contended that both the movie and its unique distribution model left a lot to be desired, proving that Christian film-makers had some work to do before they could entertain audiences on a true international stage.

From the resulting debate, two specific deductions could be made: One, the straight-to-video market works on its own, but not as advertising for a theatrical release. Two, Christian filmmakers still cannot compete with Hollywood, both in the box office and in terms of film quality. This point could be argued, as *The Passion of the Christ* debuted as a top-notch film with mega box office success, but the reality is that *The Passion* is not a Christian film, but simply a film made by a Christian. So what is meant by the term "Christian film"? In truth, the Christian film industry is still a young indie film playground with new rules and few filmmakers who are experienced enough to know the good films from the bad. Filmmakers and producers are raising money outside of the big budget studio system, and thus, films are necessarily made on the cheap.

It's the classic independent film model. A filmmaker doesn't have the money to make big movies, but he or she has a statement to make, and in the case of Christian filmmakers, a standard to uphold. Often, the most difficult circumstances bring forth the most excellent art, but this hasn't been the case for the Christian film industry ... at least, not yet.

Some have pinned the blame on message-driven films that forsake the story, while others blame the low budgets. Regardless, the Christian film industry has always been a point of dialogue and debate among Christians and Christian filmmakers. The debate kicks up in intensity every so often, especially after the disappointing box office revenue of films like *The Omega Code 2: Meggido, Left Behind, Extreme Days, Hometown Legend,* and many others, despite rising quality and depth of story with each successive project. The debate is the same one that has torn the Christian music industry for decades, producing many of the same questions: What is "Christian" film? Does a Christian filmmaker have to produce Christian films? Can movies actually be Christian? Or can a Christian filmmaker produce mainstream movies without getting flack from the Church?

Similar questions have circled these movies and others as the Christian film industry gathers momentum and begins to find a footing. Christian filmmakers often wonder: Should they produce films solely for a Christian audience, or can they tackle Hollywood with the blessing of the Church? Ultimately, this book asks the question: What can Christians do to make excellent spiritually charged films that will really impact the world?

One young, rising filmmaker has had to wrestle often these questions over the course of his career. Dallas Jenkins rides the fence between Hollywood and the Christian film industry. He produced an unusually high quality "Christian film" in *Hometown Legend*, made a short film titled *Cliché*, and is currently working on several other projects for Jenkins Entertainment. He formerly worked for Namesake Entertainment and had a role in the pre-production of *Left Behind*, though he took himself off the project before it went into production.

Many others are involved in this discussion about spirituality and film as well, including Clyde Taber, board member and former executive director of the spiritually focused Damah Film Festival; Taber's insights into this issue will help set the stage to discuss Jenkins. "The story is preeminent, and the message is within the story," Taber said. "Every story has a message because no one tells a story without a message. But the question to me is, what's preeminent? Is it the story, or is it the message? If you lose your story, oftentimes you lose your audience, because they don't care for the message any longer. If you can tell a powerful story that the message flows from, both can happen, where the story wins and the message wins."

Other Christian filmmakers say that Christians must do the hard work of learning their craft and enter the Hollywood ranks to make an impact on culture. One such voice is Monty Kelso, the director of creative communications at Coast Hills Church in Southern California. Kelso is also the founder of The Veracity Project, a filmmaking network and think tank whose goal is to train up the younger generation to change culture through film.

"Christians who penetrate secular industry and begin to influence and help secular industry rethink how and why they do what they do is probably going to be the most effective," Kelso said. "A cost culture with a Christian film tends to fall flat. Being too blatant with what we're trying to say always backfires. It just doesn't have the same effect as a more subversive approach. So taking the subversive approach in a positive way, not a hostile takeover, just being subtle and subversive in how we perpetuate the Gospel truth, I believe, is going to be the success of film in the future."

While Kelso makes great points, there are many who disagree, including Byron Jones of Garden City Pictures. "Producers have to decide, are they Christian film producers or Hollywood wannabes?" Jones said in an interview with *Christian Retailing*. "Investors need to decide that the Christian film industry is worth investing in. Many producers have tried to give the glitz of Hollywood and do a crossover film. But each time the message has been lost. The Gospel is so well hidden any sinner can watch the movie and not feel convicted. Christian films need to be less about the glitz and more about the message."[1]

Dallas Jenkins, having worked inside and outside of the Christian film industry, offers a unique insider's look.

DALLAS JENKINS

"We complain about Hollywood all the time, and yet HOLLYWOOD IS FILLED BY THOSE WHO ARE DIRECTLY OPPOSED TO OUR FAITH. They worked harder. They went to film schools; they worked their way up the system." —Dallas Jenkins

Dallas Jenkins is a man on a mission. Of late, it has become increasingly apparent that Christian filmmakers will have to try harder to make the impact they desire to make in Hollywood. Dallas Jenkins knows this. Bit by little bit, Jenkins is working to make his dent in an industry that is often described as being surrounded by impenetrable walls.

In fact, he has decided to put himself on the forefront of this movement as the president of Jenkins Entertainment, which he founded with his father, famed *Left Behind* novelist Jerry B. Jenkins. The first venture that saw Jenkins Entertainment flex its production muscle was a film called *Hometown Legend*, which did for high school football and the teenage film what *Extreme Days* did for extreme sports and teenage film. The movie tells a good story, develops some interesting characters, and even manages to weave bits of the Christian faith into the plot in subtle, not entirely distracting ways.

Jenkins said he involved himself as a producer with every detail of making *Legend*. "The director and I worked very closely together," he said. "I'm a director at heart. That's what I'm doing now and what I plan to do the rest of my life. This was an opportunity for me to learn all sides of the filmmaking process before I got into the directing end of it."

The movie, which didn't make a huge splash outside Christian circles, sought to ford the divide that currently separates Hollywood and the Christian ghetto. Many filmmakers are attempting this crossing, and while some are making good headway, Jenkins is charging full speed ahead.

Legend found video distribution with Warner Brothers, a big break for such a small movie and something even more rare for a Christian film. This partnership with Hollywood could be seen in a number of lights.

Could this be the first step in breaking down the barriers between the two industries, giving Christians more credibility? Or is this the first step toward the Christian film industry's bid as a mainstream entity that purveys its wares to secular culture?

Overall, *Legend* has been a massive learning process for Jenkins, the crew, and his company. "Our goals as a company are to make great films. We want to make the greatest films of all time," Jenkins said from his office, admitting that *Hometown Legend* probably didn't qualify. "We went into [*Hometown Legend*] hoping to do something, and we still believe we accomplished more than what many others have for their first time. And that's what we've been hearing from the industry. To get it picked up by Warner Brothers was a huge coup for us. We're very proud of it. We learned a ton. We learned everything about the business, from the script to the actual distribution, to theaters and to video."

Jenkins loves sports. Growing up, he wanted to be a professional baseball player and later a sports broadcaster. At Northwestern College, he chose to pursue a broadcasting degree and later switched his major to drama, which he earned a few years later. While working on his drama degree, he explored acting, music, and short video projects, and even directed a full-length play his senior year. But his love for film was galvanized when he saw *One Flew Over the Cuckoo's Nest*, starring Jack Nicholson, in high school.

"[That] film made me realize that I wanted to make films, I wanted to arouse emotions in the way that that movie did that for me," Jenkins said. "It really solidified when I was a freshman in college and doing some plays, and I thought, *Yeah, I've got to sell out. I can't divide my attention any other way.*"

After college, Jenkins worked for Namesake Entertainment, which was developing *Left Behind*. Some of the frustration he experienced working on the *Left Behind* project might have fueled Jenkins' next project, *Hometown Legend*, the film that launched his own film production company, Jenkins Entertainment.

"We started our own company back in January or February of 2000," Jenkins said. "We got the script for *Hometown Legend* right around that time and started developing that project, and we were shooting in October of that year."

Jenkins came across the script when he was working for Namesake. At the time, Namesake was considering the writers of *Hometown Legend* to write the *Left Behind* script. Jenkins loved the story and took the script to his dad. Both men decided to pursue it because of their love for sports, their desire to represent their faith, and their love of a good story. Jenkins said he didn't set out to make a Christian movie, but felt drawn to the story, which presented Christian themes in natural ways.

"My dad and I are huge sports fans; we're basically freaks about it," Jenkins said. "So it was a script that we liked because it was a sports script. It also had a good storyline, good character development, but then incorporated our faith in a real organic way, as opposed to a preachy, kind of tacked-on way at the end. So when we saw a script that represented our worldview was about sports and was well done, we thought, *This is a project we could start our company with.*"

If there is one thing that misfired in the making of *Hometown Legend*, Jenkins admits that the lack of star power dramatically affected the film's insignificant monetary performance. On top of that, the story, while engaging and interesting, lacks something else that often draws bigger theater interest and overall success—a compelling logline or high concept plot that is common of most studio films. While a compelling concept should never signify a film's overall success in Hollywood, and often doesn't, it is enough to generate the buzz necessary to create an underground sensation like *The Passion of the Christ*.

Jenkins said the key for Christian filmmakers is to produce a movie that has the same appeals to a mainstream audience as any other movie in the theaters. "I want Christian screenwriters to write pioneering, edgy, unique scripts that don't need any qualification as a 'Christian' or a 'secular' film," Jenkins said. "We just need to learn how to tell great stories, based on our lives, using the language of great filmmakers."[2]

THE **'CHRISTIAN'** LABEL

"It really seemed to us that this was a real under-serviced community, and PEOPLE WERE HUNGRY FOR FILM ENTERTAINMENT."
—Andre van Heerden

Can a film be "Christian"? Van Heerden, who writes, directs, produces, and consults at Cloud Ten Pictures, the most well known distributor of Christian films in North America alongside TBN, confirms that audiences respond well to the films of Cloud Ten Pictures, such as *Left Behind*, so clearly there's a demand.

To ground this discussion, it will be important to look at a host of sources that give particular insight into this issue from varying stances. Several areas of debate find this discussion at its most heated. First off, can art be Christian? Finally, are Christians compromising their ideals by making distinctly Christian art marketed directly to Christians? Conversely, are Christians compromising their ideals by making wholly mainstream or crossover art?

In his book *Of Fiction and Faith*, W. Dale Brown interviewed well-known writer and widely popular radio personality Garrison Keillor, who grew up in a fundamentalist Christian home. In their discussion of writing and faith, Brown asked Keillor if he thought there was "such a thing as a Christian writer." Keillor's response is an appropriate launch pad for this discussion.

"The writer may be a Christian, but I would hesitate to call the writings Christian writings," Keillor said in response. "I don't believe in that. 'Christian fiction' is a terrible term."[3]

While Keillor's response is likely to invoke a backlash within the Christian industry, it's important to be aware of this opinion, which is widespread among the secular academia and some Christian sophisticates.

Earlier in the same book, Brown interviews minister and Pulitzer Prize nominated novelist Frederick Buechner. Buechner's response to the same question is also fascinating and presents another view of the label.

"The reason I shy away from the phrase 'Christian writer' is that it always suggests Christian in a limited and clubbish sense," Buechner said. "I don't know if I'd want to put any adjective to myself as a writer. I'm a writer like anybody else. I do the best I can."[4]

Buechner goes on to point out how his novels tend toward spiritual themes simply because he is a religious person. It's a natural byproduct of his search for the character threads that lead his story, not necessarily his desire to evangelize his readers. Also, despite the fact that he is a member of the clergy, Buechner's books contain bad language and bad people and lots of questions, though not necessarily answers. His work seems to represent a heartfelt attempt to present an authentic story that reflects a piece of the culture in which we live.

When it comes to weighing in on this label himself, Dallas Jenkins doesn't mince words. "The term 'Christian film' has been bastardized to the point where it's only considered to be a Christian film if it's produced by a Christian production company, a company that labels themselves Christian and only distributes films to the Christian market," Jenkins said. "Then these companies decide that they're going to change Hollywood and that they're going to make movies for Christians. Unfortunately, they have not been willing to pay the same dues or pay the same money or work at the same level that non-Christians have."

It's interesting how the term "Christian" brings about such distinctions in language. Most Christians have no problem calling themselves Christians if they are followers of Jesus, but to call their artwork Christian often amounts to a paradox. Numerous so-called crossover bands have worn the Christian label at one time or another, only to shirk it and proudly move on. Why?

The truth is that the label carries a nasty stigma in a culture that is wholly unrelated to Jesus. To be associated with Christian music or Christian film is to be associated with an entire industry full of similar work and most of the time, though not always, lower quality work.

The question becomes: What is the benefit of having a distinctly "Christian" film industry? The audience is a given, so Christian films probably aren't going to be evangelistic tools, but instead, tools of encouragement. If a filmmaker slaps a Christian label on a movie, or a Christian film company produces the film, he or she risks alienating a good majority of the potential audience, and chances are very good that he or she alienates anyone who isn't a Christian already. So perhaps it's best that people consider Christian films, which are sold almost exclusively in Christian bookstores and at events, not as evangelism but as encouragement.

So where does this leave the Christian bookstores sitting in the middle of all this, trying to do an honest business with (hopefully) a quality product? Jenkins said Christian bookstores have their place and serve a valuable part of the market.

"Customers come into those stores for a specific reason," Jenkins said. "They know that what they buy, they know that there's a standard that they [can] rely on. They know that something won't offend their sensibilities."

THE CHALLENGE FOR 'CHRISTIAN' FILM

"*A Walk to Remember* was absolutely a 'Christian film,' in the sense that it had a Christian message in it. But it just happened to be produced by Warner Brothers, and so it wasn't considered a Christian film." —Dallas Jenkins

The question, "Is there such a thing as a Christian film?" will probably always be up for debate. For this book, the label doesn't fit. A Christian is a person, a follower of Christ. A film about Jesus isn't Christian, though its theology might be Christian in nature. For most purists, any form of art that is labeled Christian isn't truly art in the first place. Therefore, a film about Jesus, like Mel Gibson's *The Passion of the Christ*, is a historical biopic—or as Ralph Winter has called it, "a love poem."

The challenge now is to write, direct, and produce better movies. But in order to make better movies, filmmakers have to practice making movies—and bad ones at that. Filmmakers have to take chances and find actors and build up a collection of writing and footage and story ideas and editing equipment and contacts. They should sharpen a pencil and jot down some inspiring dialogue; read books like Robert Rodriguez's *A Rebel Without a Crew*, William Goldman's *Adventures in the Screen Trade*, or Sidney Lumet's *Making Movies*; learn screenplay format; read scripts from movies they really respect and enjoy; take a few classes. It's time for filmmakers to turn on that digital camera and roll tape on short films, documentaries, music videos, commercials, and feature films, and practice the craft of filmmaking the way they would practice anything else: by doing it.

In this mission field, when a filmmaker can change a scene in a film or make a redemptive movie in the studio system, their work doesn't just impact thousands of Christians, but millions upon millions of people. That kind of influence is rare in the world today—and should be respected by people of faith whose primary goal is to affect change in culture.

If filmmakers who call Jesus their Savior take up this challenge, they can be guaranteed a difficult road. But if filmmakers work hard enough, they can always find a way to get inside: through film festivals, contests, competitions, internships, agencies, talent firms, jobs, classes, schools, demo reels, conferences, sample scripts, and many other unique routes, independent or otherwise. The film industry may be the most formidable and competitive industry in the world, but there are thousands of avenues that lead inside.

Perseverance breeds excellence.

NOTES

1. Margaret Feinberg, "A New Era for Christian Filmmaking," *Christian Retailing*, April 19, 2004.
2. Interview with Dallas Jenkins.
3. W. Dale Brown, *Of Fiction and Faith* (Wm. B. Eerdmans, Grand Rapids, MI: 1997).
4. Ibid.

HOLLYWOOD project
FILMOGRAPHY

WRITER

Extreme Days — 2001
The Duke — 1999
Williams Syndrome:
A Highly Musical Species — 1996

DIRECTOR

Williams Syndrome:
A Highly Musical Species — 1996

HOLLYWOOD project
FILMOGRAPHY

HOLLYWOOD project
FILMOGRAPHY

05 CRAIG DETWEILER

"I think every artist, whether we call it a prayer, a wish, a hope, or a bloodletting, begins their process with a cry for inspiration. Writing is hard work. We all need to pray for imagination and inspiration every day."
—Craig Detweiler

One day, in the latter part of 2003, the indomitable Craig Detweiler stood in front of a small crowd in Hollywood, his presentation titled "Beyond Body Parts and the 'F' Word." His talk kicked off day two of a conference titled "Mere Entertainment," whose goal was to bridge the gap between those in the Church who study film and those who actually work in the film industry. During his talk, he touched on the redemptive themes found in movies like *Fight Club* and *Donnie Darko*, some tidbits of postmodern theology, and the Church's need to look beyond the harsh exterior of some of the movies coming out of Hollywood. His book, *A Matrix of Meanings: Finding God in Pop Culture*, sat on the back table, a colorful tome that seeks to discover God in music, film, sports, television, advertising, art, and even fashion.

Later that day, Detweiler led a question-and-answer discussion with the writer-director of the opening film of the City of Angels Film Festival, a popular L.A. gathering of film lovers that "explores the intersection of Film/City/Religion," according to the program, at the Directors Guild building on Sunset Boulevard. Detweiler produced the well-liked film festival and has for the past three years. In his spare time, he is also the chair of the mass communications department at Biola University in La Mirada, California.

One more thing, Detweiler is a screenwriter.

During an interview at his home in Los Angeles, Detweiler talked about his Hollywood journeys, his adventures in writing movies, and his role in training up future generations to bring excellence to the film industry and the Gospel to the world.

Detweiler's upstairs home office offers a stunning view of the Santa Monica harbor and a sprawling deck where morning coffee could last all day. During this interview, Detweiler talks about Humphrey Bogart, his favorite movies of the past few years, and *Extreme Days*, the most well-known film he's worked on. The film was a triumph for many, but considered a failure to some because it accomplished all its goals—save one. It failed to score a significant box office tally, though it entertained young audiences across the country and is still shown widely in youth groups everywhere. Unfortunately, the Hollywood monarchy, fairly or unfairly, dismissed the film.

Detweiler has since moved on and extended his reach and influence by working on a book, speaking across the country, teaching classes, and even writing a few more screenplays to soak up his off-hours. On top of that, he's involved in a host of ambitious projects all over Hollywood, from writing schools to conferences, where he continues to influence young filmmakers, writers, and theologians with his own brand of studied passion for excellent cinema.

But how did all this happen? How did he go from being just a guy who loved movies to becoming a widely connected, well-respected Christian screenwriter, speaker, and theologian in the Hollywood arena? The answer can be summed up in just a few words: schooling, hard work, and an agreement with his wife.

"When I graduated USC [University of Southern California], my wife basically gave me five years," Detweiler said with a smirk. "She said, 'I'll support us for five years, and you practice your craft. But by the year 2000, it's all on you, buddy.' So I stayed at home and wrote. Within about a year of graduating from USC, I sold my first script."

THE **EVOLUTION** OF **DETWEILER**

"THE COST OF PAPER IS CHEAPER THAN THE COST OF FILM. So I chose the emphasis in screenwriting." —Craig Detweiler

Craig Detweiler has always loved movies. When he realized that there were actually regular people, who put their pants on one leg at a time, making movies for a living, he thought to himself, *Hey, I could do that!*

Humphrey Bogart is his earliest memory of film. The iconic man's man of early Hollywood personified for him what it meant to be a man. Movies also gave him his first on-screen image of Jesus, who he remembers thinking of as a cool, uncompromising, and loyal hero. "All my pre-categories for Jesus were laid by film," Detweiler said, describing the Jesus of the movies as "Bogart and beyond."

"I think it took a while for me to give myself permission to love movies as a person of faith," Detweiler said. "Once I did, once I realized that the things I loved could be things that God loves, I was free to actually start to create and to write and to be truly kind of an integrated person. Seminary was a part of that."

Detweiler first went to graduate school at Fuller Seminary in Pasadena, California, where he obtained a Master of Divinity degree. The logical next step for seminary graduates is a one-way ticket into a ministry of one sort or another. But Detweiler took another route and in doing so, represented a move that has become very common to the younger generation of creative spiritual seekers. People everywhere are digging up new career forums in which to demonstrate their faith, serve people, react to God creatively, and worship, while ministering to the world.

As this idea bounds the globe, springing up in Europe with co-ops and churches starting up in clubs, movie theaters, and pubs, Hollywood itself is surging with filmmakers of faith like Detweiler, who are seeking to impact culture via the most powerful medium on earth. This phenomenon could be attributed to a kind of whiplash reaction to the structuralism of the previous generation, or conversely, it may be due in part to the previous generation's encouragement, as was the case in Detweiler's experience.

"I had a professor at seminary who taught theology and culture and probably should have been a film director—that was truly his first love," Detweiler said. "I think he didn't feel he had permission to pursue the arts as a person of faith. In his class, I sort of heard the challenge that if you feel an inkling in that way, you'd be a fool not to pursue it. I clearly heard, I think, the call of God to go to film school, to pursue the movies."

So it was that Craig Detweiler emerged from Fuller Seminary, a missionary headed for a truly postmodern mission field. Soon after, he was accepted into the USC's prestigious film production program, where he studied film production, with an emphasis in screenwriting, for two intense years.

While at USC, Detweiler also wrote and directed a documentary titled *Williams Syndrome: A Highly Musical Species* for a Dutch television station on which it later aired. The film profiles kids who have Williams Syndrome, a rare condition that boosts a person's musical and language skills, though they might lack other social or intellectual faculties.

"I stumbled across an article in the *L.A. Times* while I was in film school," he said. "You have these kids—I would almost call them musical savants—who, if they've heard an Italian opera, might be able to reproduce it for you. I was working for a Dutch television network at the time. So while I was in film school, working on the side, I was getting paid professionally to write, direct, and produce my first documentary."

The film went on to win the Crystal Heart Award at the Heartland Film Festival and the CINE Golden Eagle. And while Detweiler loves screenwriting, what he really wants to do is direct films, not an uncommon ambition in Hollywood—and in Studio City, Santa Monica, Culver City, and the rest of Los Angeles for that matter.

A funny old adage repeated over and over in writing classes everywhere is "write what you know." Detweiler had heard this saying before, but after graduating from USC, he threw that advice out the window and started a spec script called *The Duke* about a dog who inherits his British master's title and fortune.

"I've never had a dog, and I'm not part of British royalty," Detweiler said laughing. "I went for the completely ridiculous, the craziest thing you could dream up, and the silliest poster you can imagine. And that's why it sold, I think."

It was later that year that Detweiler finished up his unlikely script and began to shop it around to potential buyers. He got the script in the hands of the people who produced Disney's *Air Bud*, and suddenly they were interested in making the film.

"I think [the producers] could immediately see the poster. Dog, crown, I get it. I know how to sell this movie," he said. "So I wrote one movie for like eight-year-olds, another movie for fourteen-year-olds, and I'm working my way up. The next thing I want to do is a college film."

The Disney Channel produced *The Duke*, where it is shown periodically. The film can also be found in your local video store, sporting a cover that features a stately looking dog wearing a crown and sitting on a velvet throne.

EXTREME DAYS

"ALMOST EVERY WEEK, I HEAR FROM SOMEBODY who says, 'I can't get that soundtrack off my kid's CD player,' or, 'He makes us watch such-and-such a scene over and over and over. And you know, it's very gratifying that the film continues to live on, on the small screen."
—Craig Detweiler

Extreme Days hit theaters (and later released to home video where it became hugely popular) on the heels of a whole slew of lackluster Christian films that had given mainstream audiences the impression that Christian filmmakers were untalented, unfunny, uncreative, and less than technically savvy. *Extreme Days* bore the brunt of this stigma when theatergoers ignored the movie on its opening weekend. But the quality of a film is not measured by its box office rank alone.

Detweiler and his co-writer Eric Hannah, who also directed the film, wrote *Extreme Days* to be a fun teenage comedy with a heart, leaving out all graphic innuendo and tenuous sexual content while preserving the craziness of an extreme sports-themed movie. At its essence, the film was a response to films like *American Pie*, *Road Trip*, and a host of other teenage comedies that had done massive business but overflowed with crude humor and an overwhelming host of questionable messages directed at teens.

When the *Extreme Days* project began gaining momentum in the late '90s, people described it as a project whose status was up in the air. The shoot had been scheduled, the crew was in place, and distribution was ready to go. From early reports, the project was an ambitious effort to give youth culture something fresh, as the film featured extreme sports, a road trip storyline, and a young cast. Hannah knew what he wanted the picture to be about, he had a schedule and crew, and he even had a fairly substantial budget. But he didn't have the key element to actually make the film a reality: The script had not yet been written in its entirety.

Enter Craig Detweiler.

"I heard they were looking for a writer," he said. "Eric called up a program called Act One: Writing for Hollywood. He said he was looking for a hip, young, edgy screenwriter. Well, for the oddest of reasons, they recommended me (laughs). Even though I was none of those things."

Detweiler went down for an interview with Hannah, and the two hit it off immediately. "Some of his first questions were, 'Do you skate, snowboard, or you know, hang glide?' And my answer was, 'No, I ski. A little bit.' I think he actually was intrigued by the honesty of that, that I wasn't trying to make myself look 'extreme.' But as a writer, you can still, hopefully, enter into the experience of almost anybody."

Hannah hired Detweiler soon after the initial interview, and the two men began having regular writing sessions to work on the script. "One of [Eric's] hopes was to deal with the question of abstinence and to put that out there as a possibility," Detweiler said. "And I was fine with that, but I wanted it to be a person who came to a stance of abstinence through sexual experience. So that really, wherever you were in your life and in your life experience as an audience member, you could relate to this girl."

As the story began to evolve, Hannah decided that the movie would focus on a road trip, which would allow for a number of extreme sports detours and comedic road trip gags. Hannah also knew from the outset that he wanted the story to follow two brothers, their friends, and a girl, a structure loosely based on his own life experience in meeting his wife.

The resulting film is full of skateboarding, surfing, snowboarding, and motorcross moments, hilarious, if contrived, teen comedy sketches, and a dash of romance that doesn't sink into sentimentalism. Hannah and Detweiler also achieved their balance of honesty and sensitivity in conveying the message of abstinence. The quality of the acting was solid, and the actors, though mostly unknown, possessed the kind of charisma necessary for the film to gain a massive youth group following on video and DVD.

In many Christian circles in which expectation for any overtly Christian film is understandably low, *Extreme Days* was universally loved. One Christian reviewer called the film "the best intentionally Christian film ever made, bar none." But still, the mainstream film industry roundly ignored *Extreme Days*, and its disappointing box office bow signified either secular disinterest or marketing avenues that simply didn't work in mainstream culture.

BEYOND BODY PARTS AND THE F-WORD

"I'm consistently thrilled by what the next generation of filmmakers is producing. At the core, THEIR FILMS ARE LOADED WITH THEOLOGICAL QUESTIONS AND SPIRITUAL SEARCHING, whether they're conscious of it or not." —Craig Detweiler

Back at the conference, Detweiler told an audience of aspiring screenwriters, theologians, youth pastors, and filmmakers that this generation doesn't truly have a great war. He said, "Our great war is a spiritual war."

He went on to cite a list of films that have helped define the paradoxical issues with which this generation is grappling. During the interview
at his home office, he went on to describe these films as powerhouses
whose spiritual intensity is indicative of the spiritual intensity of this
generation.

The list included movies such as *Fight Club*, *Dogma*, *Magnolia*, and *Donnie Darko*. Detweiler also talked about *American Beauty*, the disturbing,
Academy Award-winning film written by gay screenwriter Alan Ball. In
the movie, which was unanimously loved by secular audiences despite
its (or perhaps because of) its questionable material, there is a gorgeous
scene in which the main characters watch a video of a plastic bag float-
ing on the wind for what might have been ten minutes. In some ways,
the scene is the centerpiece of the movie, a moment that attempts to
capture the hints of a higher power that we all sense from time to time.

"When Alan Ball won his Oscar for best screenplay, he had this long list
of people that he thanked," Detweiler said. "People that inspired him,
teachers, and he ended it by thanking the plastic bag that danced with
him outside the World Trade Center in a time when he really needed
it. And so that central scene about the benevolent force that gives us no
reason to fear and reminds us that there's goodness in the world, that
was a real trade-center moment out of his own life. And [onstage] he
thanked that benevolent force that revealed itself to him that day."

This seeming paradox, that finds a gay screenwriter thanking God
within the confines of such a liberal and spiritually averse industry,
is now the postmodern standard. This example is encouraging for its
acknowledgement of God, and discouraging because of its simultaneous
embracing of moral relativism.

But based on Detweiler's conclusion about film's significance, it becomes more and more obvious that film is the moral touchstone bringing about the most intense spiritual dialogue within this and future
generations, as the Church stands and watches. While the Church is the

most vital institution in all of Christendom, the emerging generation's tendency to seek out alternative methods for seeking God should motivate us to make better movies, or at least incorporate film more often into our churches.

In the endeavor to make better movies, Detweiler offers this advice to filmmakers: "Don't spoil the film by trying to over-explain everything. Maintain the mystery."

Perhaps Detweiler's work will pave the way for filmmakers who want to make morally and spiritually uplifting films in the mainstream marketplace. Clearly he is making a significant impact in the Church, in academia, and in Hollywood itself. But how does Craig Detweiler deal with moving beyond the simplistic Christian label in his own career?

"I understand that I've got to pay the price for those who've gone before, you know, guilt by association," Detweiler said. "But, hopefully, I'm making the way easier so that twenty years from now, the next generation of filmmakers will be inspired to tell a lot more. I hope *Extreme Days* was a small step forward in moving people of faith toward excellence, honesty, and intelligent truth in whatever form."

HOLLYWOOD project
FILMOGRAPHY

WRITER

The In-Laws — 2003
Levity — 2003
Charlie's Angels — 2000
What Planet Are You From? — 2000
The Unbelieveables (TV) — 1999
Men in Black — 1997

Super Mario Bros. — 1993
Mom and Dad Save the World — 1992
Leaving Normal — 1992
Bill & Ted's Bogus Journey — 1991
Bill & Ted's Excellent Adventure — 1989
It's the Garry Shandling Show (TV) — 1986

PRODUCER

Levity — 2003
Chief — 2000
The Garden — 2000
Jordeys — 2000
The Unbelievables (TV) — 1999
Leaving Normal — 1992
Bill & Ted's Bogus Journey — 1991

DIRECTOR

Levity — 2003
The Unbelievables (TV) — 1999

HOLLYWOOD project
FILMOGRAPHY

ED SOLOMON

⊠ THE GRAVITY OF GUILT

"You could just reach your arm out and punch somebody and affect their life forever. You're often just a split second, at any time, away from dramatically altering the course of somebody else's life." —Ed Solomon

12:35 p.m.: It is the Los Angeles press day for a small independent film called *Levity*.

Ed Solomon escorts Holly Hunter through the lobby of a high-profile Beverly Hills hotel, complete with rangy, cell phone-sporting publicity folk and an array of important-looking, or at least well-dressed, people. Today he wears a dark collared shirt, while Hunter wears a trim blouse cut off at the sleeves, showing off defined, muscular arms. The writer-director and the starlet stride into an overlarge banquet room that has been rapidly transformed into a press gallery with a round table and a few chairs. The room feels big and empty as they sit down quickly to face a panel of quote-hungry reporters and writers. His face lights up and she smiles; they're ready to answer questions, any questions.

Before Solomon has had the chance to pull up his chair, the first question is fired off, all pleasantries obviously aside. At this point they bristle, both of them, and faces become serious; smile creases give way to forehead creases, furrowed eyebrows, and frowns of concentration. Thankfully, they appear to be seasoned veterans when it comes to the press, and they take it all in stride.

"Where did you get the idea to write *Levity*?" Ten reporters pull out tape recorders and press "record" in unison as Solomon answers.

"When I was in college, I tutored at a prison for kids who committed violent crimes," he says slowly, choosing his words carefully, though he's told this story many times. "One of the kids I worked with had killed somebody. He was tried as an adult and sentenced to life in prison. I remember he kept reaching into his pocket to pull out this photograph, and he'd turn it over, close it up, and put it back. And he did this continuously. I had this image of him staring at this two-dimensional photograph, hoping for some kind of three-dimensional story of this person's life, so he could comprehend what he had done. And this image of the boy in the photograph stayed with me."

When Solomon set out to write *Levity* some years ago, he knew this was a movie he wanted to direct. The consummate Hollywood comedy writer got some of the movie industry's finest actors to read the script (after countless studio rejections), including Billy Bob Thornton, Morgan Freeman, Kirsten Dunst, and Hunter, all of whom loved the story and subsequently attached themselves to star in the film. Soon after, he signed Roger Deakins to shoot the film. After aligning himself with an incredibly talented Hollywood cast and crew, Solomon set out to make his directorial debut.

As Solomon continues to work the press gallery, his replies are quick: He listens intently and then answers, looking down at the table frequently while he talks, using his hands to emphasize this point or that. His short and neatly trimmed graying hair had been a mop of curls only months before while on the set of *Levity*, which was filmed in a snowy Toronto, Canada. Solomon describes the production journey as harrowing, difficult, and stressful, the experience of a lifetime. He is asked about the themes of guilt and redemption, which are the strongest undercurrents of his film. He is also asked about the title and how it seems to run contrary to the movie's major heavy themes. "I wanted to call the movie *Levity* because of its relation to both laughter, things which elevate the human spirit, and lightness," he said. "But I tried to design the film so that it would have silence. There's a moment where Holly and Billy just sit there, and there are times when Billy's just sitting. I wanted people to put themselves into the film. It can work really well for some people, and it can enrage others who go, 'Why aren't you entertaining me at this juncture!' or whatever. Like the movie has to be multitasking."

For a movie that moves slowly (one reviewer called it "glacial" in its pace) and deals with issues of despair and pain in all of its major and supporting characters, *Levity* is surely an unexpected title. The paradox of the film rests in this idea of levity, which is something that pursues each character relentlessly, haunting them on the periphery, just out of sight and out of reach. The movie is a powerful drama and gives weighty performance a new standard.

Holly Hunter is immediately striking, and she is much shorter than she ever appears on film. Also, she speaks with unique power and a thoughtful intelligence that forms the basis of her onscreen charisma. Her charming Southern drawl peals through her famous cracked half-smile that has been seen on the screen numerous times. She answers questions quickly and seems well accustomed to the questions she's asked, as if she has anticipated them before they come. The question this time: "What attracted you to this character and to the project?"

After a moment of pause, Hunter begins to speak about her character's sense of mystery. "It's something that I encounter rarely," she continues. "Although that happened with *The Piano*, where I was introduced to the fact that mystery could be inherent in a character on the page, because everyone is mysterious, everyone is a little inexplicable. Generally, movies distill things down to answers. This one doesn't, and that, I'm sure, attracted all of us to the story."

Levity is not a Hollywood film. Some critics have called it an overly depressing portrait of a man in search of relief from a lifetime of guilt. Some critics have called it a quiet, moving story told with an understated grace.

The film's early scenes are haunting and slow-moving, punctuated by a subdued tone that is disconcerting. The main character, Manual, lives in a strange, beautiful, and spiritually rich void, and very slowly, the viewer is pulled into his story. This character embodies paradox. Sitting before a parole board in the beginning of the movie, he tells his judges that he feels guilty for his crime and is content to stay jailed. After being released, he searches for forgiveness, but he doesn't believe in the God that can give it to him. Manual acknowledges this up front in a candid engaging voice-over. How can a man acknowledge that he needs forgiveness from a higher power, but remain unconvinced of the idea of God? This story begs the question, What is going on in this filmmaker's mind? The next question that lurches to mind is, How can spiritually concerned filmmakers make more movies that reflect the depth of longing or the depth of subtext that haunts this beautiful story?

WHO IS **ED SOLOMON?**

"Just like you listen to different kinds of music, you go to different kinds of movies, you read different kinds of books, for different reasons. I think ONE WRITES DIFFERENT KINDS OF THINGS FOR DIFFERENT REASONS." —Ed Solomon

Ed Solomon's directorial debut marked a huge departure in style for the man who, up to this point, was best known for writing the box-office smashes *Men In Black*, *Bill and Ted's Excellent Adventure*, and *Bill and Ted's Bogus Journey*. Most had pigeonholed Solomon as someone who exclusively wrote commercial, big-idea comedy, but since the beginning of his career, writing has always been about much more than just a paycheck.

"I was kind of an insecure kid who, like many kids, just felt utterly detached from people," Solomon said on the phone from a New York hotel room. "Writing, to me, always seemed like a bridge between myself and others. I didn't realize it at the time, that you're connecting while keeping distance, which is why it was so comfortable to me."

It all started with comedy. Solomon began writing jokes and sketches for comedians when he was just a teenager. While in college at UCLA, Solomon also frequented Los Angeles comedy clubs, where he started writing jokes on the fly for comedians looking to work new sketches into their acts. He started writing jokes after trying his hand at doing stage comedy himself and found that it was harder than it looked.

Solomon also began to write for the theater during this time and managed to hammer out seven stage plays. In his senior year of college, he got a staff job on *Laverne and Shirley*, although he said of the job, "I wasn't that good at it."

When a fellow student by the name of Chris Matheson directed Solomon's one-act play *The Last Angel*, the two hit it off and created an improvisation workshop where the characters Bill and Ted were born. The genesis for what was going to be Solomon's big break began in various sketches about two high school losers who were studying history although they had no concept of historical events or figures. Years later, Solomon assesses his work by the quality of the final product. For example, on his own scale, Solomon approves of only fifteen minutes of *Bill and Ted's Bogus Journey*, two-thirds of *Men in Black*, and just three episodes of *It's the Garry Shandling Show*. He likes the sweet tone of *Bill and Ted's Excellent Adventure*, but wishes some of the more outlandish scenes had been left in the script and, subsequently, the movie.

"Everything I've written on assignment, except for *Men in Black*, I've ultimately been ashamed of the final product, the film," he said, "because every time, it's someone else's idea, and they already have preconceived notions of what they want it to be, so you're essentially fulfilling their vision of it. I don't personally consider myself a real writer when I'm doing that."

When asked to rate *Levity* on the same scale, Solomon deferred.

"I'm not the type that feels satisfied with one's work," he said. "I don't think I'll be able to know for a long time how I ultimately feel about [*Levity*]. I'm going through a phase where I'm not watching it anymore, because I'm only seeing the flaws now. I'm trying to avoid the headache that comes with that. You can't ever judge your own work. Whether something's successful or not, in its own sort of time frame, you have to wait until you've got distance."

Since Solomon's star has risen, he has racked up such an impressive rap sheet of credited and uncredited script rewrites that it's a wonder he had time to fit in a film like *Levity*. The list includes *X-Men* and *The In-Laws*, and he was one of numerous writers on the first *Charlie's Angels* movie. Other writing credits from his career include *Leaving Normal*, *Mom and Dad Save the World* (with Chris Matheson), *Super Mario Brothers*, and the Garry Shandling star vehicle *What Planet Are You From?*

LEARNING FROM LEVITY

"I tried to keep a level of mystery ... I THOUGHT THERE WOULD BE MORE RESONANCE IF THERE WERE LESS ANSWERS GIVEN, more questions posed, and more complex notes hit." —Ed Solomon

Levity opens on the face of Manual Jordan (Billy Bob Thornton). He wears a long mop of straight, gray hair as he sits in front of a parole board; his face is blank and worn; his expression is noteworthy only because of its lack of anything resembling emotion. The parole board tells him he is going to be let free, but it doesn't register on his face; in fact, for a few moments, he doesn't get it, saying he doesn't want to be let free.

Moments later, Manual walks out of prison a free man and looks lost. He wanders through the subway and the streets; he looks overwhelmed in the bustling crowd. In one moment, he stands still against a wall in a subway station, dumbstruck by life as masses of people swirl around and past him. And for much of the film's first act, Manual wanders around, unsure of himself and of what he's doing in the world. He begins to speak in voice-over, saying that he doesn't believe in God, but confirms that he feels the need to be forgiven by God or by somebody for murdering a boy more than twenty years before. In his thoughts, Manual concludes that he is doomed to accept a life lived in guilt, or just doomed to live life without forgiveness.

"Billy Bob's character, Manual, says, 'I don't believe in redemption for myself. I don't believe in God. I do not deserve to be forgiven, and I don't want to be in the world,'" Solomon said, touching on the stark spirituality of the movie. "And then he's put there. It's much more challenging. If I had made this film about a character who believes in God, who gets out of jail, you know where he'd go. It's a tougher burden for someone who doesn't believe in God because the answers aren't laid out in front of you."

What makes this film's character unique? Is it his burden of guilt and simultaneously irrepressible need for forgiveness from God? Is it his atheism that leaves him denying the existence of God, while craving more connection with the world? In truth, this character isn't all that unique in Hollywood, but would a Christian filmmaker make a film about an atheist looking for forgiveness without finding God? Solomon's plot line allows for several fruitful irresolutions that wouldn't exist if the movie wrapped itself up with Manual's finding answers in God at the end of the film.

Looking at this film gives more insight into both an atheist and an ag-
nostic view of forgiveness. It's especially interesting to note that Solomon thinks believers in God have all the answers laid out in front of
them, that they know where they would go in Manual's predicament. It
might be truer to say that all humans—Christian, Muslim, atheist, agnos-
tic, or otherwise—are plagued with questions, guilt, sincere moments of
faith, and long journeys where faith is lacking. Soon after the introduction, *Levity* asks questions not only of its characters, but of its audience
as well. Almost immediately, the viewers are forced to make a decision:
Either invest in these characters, or opt out of learning from this film
altogether. And this is why *Levity* is so successful. Viewers either have to
sit tight and start rooting for Manual to find forgiveness from his massive
burden or put their hopes in waiting for the flashy action scene or riot-
ous one-liner that never shows up.

And so it begins. *Levity* opens with such a dour feeling of hopelessness
that it is no wonder some viewers and even some critics immediately
opted out. The film continues along hopelessly, following Manual as he
wanders aimlessly through a nondescript city. When Manual picks up a
ringing pay phone, he meets Miles Evans (Morgan Freeman), a grouchy
preacher who runs a ramshackle center to feed the homeless and the
poor. They meet and strike up a loose friendship. At the center, Miles
allows patrons of a local nightclub to park in his parking lot, and in
exchange, they listen to him preach for fifteen minutes. In those fifteen
minutes, Miles preaches on all things biblical to an audience of half a
dozen kids or fewer, who are constantly checking their watches and taking off mid-sermon when their fifteen minutes are up.

Manual is quickly recruited as Miles' parking lot attendant and janitor in
exchange for room and board. While on the job, Manual makes friends
with the young and reckless Sofia Mellinger (Kirsten Dunst), a formerly
rich musician's daughter whose late night drug binges result in her passing out, forcing Manual to take her home one night. Later the two talk
and become friends, as Manual tries to get her to give up her destructive
lifestyle.

It isn't long before Manual begins to seek out the forgiveness that has eluded him for years. He goes out of his way to make friends with Adele Easley (Holly Hunter), who is actually the sister of the boy he killed twenty-three years earlier. Without knowing anything about him or his past, Adele is charmed by the awkward and polite ex-con, and she sees him as a good influence on her rebellious teenage son, Abner.

Solomon explained why he had Manual seek out Adele midway through the film. "I was trying to explore these ideas about somebody whose actions really mattered in a huge way, even though they were quick and inexplicable," he said. "He just inexplicably pulled the trigger and took a human being off the planet. I thought, Well, what are the results of that action? Who does he affect?"

Clearly the person affected most by the tragedy is Adele, but Manual doesn't tell her anything about his past, and somehow the two become close friends in a very short amount of time. What is unclear at this stage is whether Manual will come clean and tell Adele who he is.

From here, Manual helps Sofia, encouraging her to give up the drugs. He isn't the father she never had, but he's close enough, and when she joins a group of after-school kids he's working with, she begins to grow into responsibility. He and Adele fall into a close relationship that is marked by moments of tenderness and awkward but innocent situations. He even goes out of his way to help her son by sitting him down in a diner and talking to him about the consequences of his destructive actions. Her son doesn't listen, but we get the feeling that Manual is making giant leaps in character he wouldn't have been prone to a few weeks before.

The most curious character of the film is Miles, the passionate parking-lot preacher. He feeds the homeless, preaches in the evenings, and even helps Manual to start an after school program. He dispenses sage-like advice with a gravelly voice and a smirk. The contrast between Manual, who is weighed down by the constant search for forgiveness, and Miles, who is doing so much good while harboring his own hidden flaws, is a beautiful portrait of complex humanity in all its destructive richness.

Levity could very easily be seen as a satire of the human condition, showing how we all are equally beautiful and flawed at the core of ourselves, whether preacher or convict, drug-addicted teenager or single mom. This kind of a statement provides a wonderful backdrop for the themes of guilt and redemption that permeate Manual's life.

In the film's conclusion, a series of events unfold that wrap up the primary plot lines. The final interaction between Adele and Manual shows for the first time in the film how deeply Adele was affected by her brother's death. This scene also confirms the possibility of forgiveness in this life, even for someone who has committed murder, though suggesting that redemption might come at a cost. By this point, Manual has completed a kind of Greek hero's journey, in which he has lived through a near-death experience and has made it back from the foreign land with the prize. In the case of this story, the prize, in the Greek myth sense, represents freedom from the weight of his guilt—or levity.

In most films, there is a key image that often symbolizes a character's flaw or current state of mind. At the end of many films, that key image is either seen as having renewed worth, or it is left behind as the character moves on with his or her life. When the key image is left behind, often this symbolizes a growth of character or a releasing of a burden. For example, in the movie *Titanic*, the key image is a diamond necklace called the Heart of the Ocean. In *The Salton Sea*, starring Val Kilmer, the key image is a trumpet.

In *Levity*, the key image is a yellowed newspaper clipping of the boy Manual murdered twenty-two years earlier. Like Solomon's story of the boy he tutored while in college, Manual carries this picture with him everywhere and looks at it often. He even posts it on the wall in his room at Miles' center. For the audience, this is a constant reminder of Manual's mindset and the guilt he carries. In one of the final scenes,

Manual leaves the center, while the yellowed newspaper clipping still hangs taped to the wall, symbolizing his shedding of the guilt he carried for so long.

This film is a great illustration of how to address spiritual issues while skirting didacticism. Many films trying desperately to portray a story of spiritual relevance descend into preachy messages or pretension. But the characters in *Levity* maintain a duality that makes them interesting and beautiful to watch, despite their painful humanity. Throughout the film, the audience comes to realize that each person onscreen has his or her fatal flaws, dents, and scratches. When a movie's characters spit out perfect dialogue and run around completing two-dimensional tasks with no sense of depth or frailty, the film itself loses a level of humanity that must be inherent in effective stories. Characters with depth (i.e., characters that are royally screwed up) imply reality, which means the audience will better relate to the movie as a whole.

Stories with flawed characters also allow an opportunity to point out how God can demonstrate His grace every day. In the book of 2 Corinthians in the Bible, the Apostle Paul asks God to take away his weakness. But God replies, "My grace is sufficient for you, for my power is made perfect in weakness." Paul then says, "Therefore I will boast all the more gladly about my weaknesses, so that Christ's power may rest on me. That is why, for Christ's sake, I delight in weaknesses, in insults, in hardships, in persecutions, in difficulties. For when I am weak, I am strong."

In terms of storytelling, it becomes clear right away that Solomon intends to tell a true story. He doesn't break out a Magic Marker and a piece of billboard-sized cardboard so he can post his preconceived message for the world to see. Instead, Solomon focuses on the resolution of his character's story arc, which is Manual's need for forgiveness, instead of tackling the other issues and questions the film brings to mind. And there are some whoppers—Is there a God? Is it possible to reform a murderer? Can a preacher still be effective if he's hiding a dark secret? There are no easy answers to these questions, and Solomon doesn't attempt to answer them either. He simply uses these issues as sounding boards for Manual's personal journey, the true centerpiece of the story. Spiritual films too often run amuck when they lose focus, stray from the main character's story, and beat the drums of a message that isn't the true center of the film. When asked to comment on asking questions without answering them, Solomon said, "I think the more you spoon-feed people, the less resonance it has."

Levity is also an exploration of the idea that redemption is possible whether or not someone believes in God. Like the story of the prodigal son in Luke 15, God gives everyone second chances; this theme, coming directly from someone who says he doesn't even know if God can exist, is extremely convincing. This is one of many examples from Hollywood in which someone outside the faith can impact the Church and the world with a story that has spiritual intensity and power.

But what about Ed Solomon himself? How much of his spiritual life is rooted in the character of Manual? Did Solomon write this film to purge the spiritual struggles inside his own heart? It isn't uncommon for art to imitate life in this way, and it is said that the best writers bleed on the page.

SOLOMON'S SPIRITUALITY

"As individuals, I think WE OFTEN FEEL THAT NOTHING WE DO MAKES ANY DIFFERENCE, that our actions don't matter." —Ed Solomon

Solomon wrote *Levity* over several years and then took a couple years to actually produce the film. In Hollywood, the vast majority of film scripts are never produced, and of the films that are made, most never see the light of day due to something often simply referred to as "development hell."

So why was Solomon so determined to put *Levity* on the big screen? "It kept returning to me, in my mind, as something not to shelf," he said. "Sometimes when I finish something and nobody wants it, I don't return to it because I got a feeling that the reason they don't want it is because they're right. This time I feel like they're not right, and I felt like I really wanted this one to happen."

People on a spiritual search are fascinating no matter what they find, and Solomon's own spiritual travels are no exception. Where is Solomon at in his faith journey to have made a film with such a strong statement of redemption? "I don't have a clear sense of faith," he shared. "I struggle. I kind of feel like when you're riding your bike on the side of the road, almost falling off the shoulder and almost staying on the cement, and you keep trying to stay on the cement. I feel like I'm sort of teetering between agnosticism and atheism, Buddhism and Judaism. I just don't know where I'm at, and I've never been able to have either an inner experience to tell me that something is right or an external experience to tell me that something is right."

Clearly, *Levity*'s spiritual wrestling match has been birthed from these very struggles. Yet it should be noted that *Levity* contains its fair share of bad language. Does that mean Christians should not recommend the film, even though it might force those who don't know God to think about Him? Again, it's hard to deny that God can speak truth through those who don't believe in Him, just as he spoke to Israel through the Assyrians, or that non-Christians can unconsciously identify so power-fully with God's truth that they are forced to send these truths back into the world. It's too easy to simply discount a film for its rating or its worldview.

Romans 1:19-20 makes it clear that we can't limit or fully understand how or to whom God will reveal Himself: "For the truth about God is known to them instinctively. God has put this knowledge in their hearts. From the time the world was created, people have seen the earth and sky and all that God made. They can clearly see his invisible qualities—

his eternal power and divine nature. So they have no excuse whatsoever for not knowing God."

A particularly insightful review was printed in the *San Francisco Chronicle* the week the film was released. Reviewer Mick LaSalle made this observation: "Solomon's agnosticism on the subjects of atonement and redemption—the precise areas of the film's investigation—makes the filmmaker as paralyzed as his lead character. If Solomon believed, *Levity* might have been stirring. If he disbelieved, it might have been chilling. Instead, *Levity* is locked into a ruminative mode. Because the filmmaker, though caring about the issues he presents, has come to no resolution, his film can end only in the nowhere zone of ambiguity and emotional limbo."[1] LaSalle and his article make a strong statement against spiritual indecision. But it is precisely this indecision that gives *Levity* such weight. Manual Jordan approaches the world after prison feeling hopeless, and to some extent, it appears that Solomon takes this approach as well. Looking at *Levity* as a primer on the bleak worldview held by some non-Christians, it's possible to learn a lot about having more compassion for those in the world.

Solomon finished his thoughts on spirituality and God with these words: "So I'm just kind of living in this world and trying to live ethically and with a sense of compassion. That being said, I think I feel a burden, a weight, a sense of guilt, a sense of fear and a sense of loneliness."

This is a vulnerable thing for someone to say, especially in Hollywood, but on a deeply personal level, it's not hard to understand what he means.

NOTES

1. Mick LaSalle, "His Baggage Is Heavy, Man Killer Caught in Limbo in Quest for Redemption," *San Francisco Chronicle*, April 11, 2003.

WRITER

Land of Plenty — 2004
Ghosting — 2001
Urban Legends: Final Cut — 2000
Hellraiser: Inferno — 2000
Dracula 2000 (Uncredited Rewrite) — 1999
Love in the Ruins — 1995

DIRECTOR

Ghosting — 2001
Hellraiser: Inferno — 2000
Love in the Ruins — 1995

HOLLYWOOD project
FILMOGRAPH

HOLLYWOOD project
FILMOGRAPHY

HOLLYWO

HOLLYWOOD project
FILMOGRAPHY

SCOTT DERRICKSON

HELLRAISER AS SCREWTAPE

"I got interested in film at a very early age because I come from a family that was pretty obsessive about movie watching, and I saw a lot of movies growing up. In fact, my family at times would see as many as three movies in a day."
—Scott Derrickson

The *Hellraiser* horror film franchise is known for its over-the-top violence, cardboard characters, and plot lines so dull that it's hard to imagine anyone steering it in the right direction. But Christian filmmaker Scott Derrickson isn't one to let a challenge pass him by. In the late '90s, Dimension Films offered Derrickson the chance to write and direct the fifth film in the bloody series. Armed with C.S. Lewis as inspiration, he took the job, seeing it as an opportunity to give the horror genre a needed creative revision, while at the same time injecting the horror film with a redemptive theme.

Dimension Films had just acquired the rights to the *Hellraiser* franchise and were shopping for story ideas among young Hollywood writers. Derrickson had recently sold a spec script called *Darkness Falling* to Tristar Pictures. Unfortunately, Columbia had just acquired Tristar, and the new boss "didn't understand" *Darkness Falling*. In effect, the script went into turnaround (a nice way of saying it was shelved), and suddenly, Derrickson had a bit of time on his hands. Then Dimension Films came calling.

"They called and asked if I was interested. So I watched all four of the [movies], and I said, 'Pass,'" Derrickson said with a laugh. "I really wasn't interested, and then I got an idea for how that movie could end. But I never called them about it."

A few weeks later, Derrickson got a call from his agent who heard that Dimension Films had gone out to twelve or thirteen other writers and passed on all of their ideas. "'They want to know if you have any ideas at all,'" Derrickson said, quoting his agent. "I said, 'Well, yeah, I've got this one, but it's like a detective movie, and I don't think they'll want to do it.' He said, 'Well, go meet with them anyway.' So I was like, 'Okay,' and I drove there, and I threw it out to them. They said, 'That's the best *Hellraiser* idea ever,' at which point, I drove home and called the Writers Guild to see if I could write under a pseudonym." He laughed again.

What Derrickson pitched to the Dimension executives that day became the fifth installment in a line of *Hellraiser* films that, unlike its predecessors, was notable for its mix of graphic horror, subtle thriller, and overt psychological drama. From the beginning, Derrickson set out to achieve a higher standard and make more than just a grisly horror movie. His goal was decidedly challenging: He had to tell a smart horror story that reflected his passion for excellence and his values, while packing a fiery punch that true horror film fans would still enjoy. And all of this had to be accomplished with a budget of less than $2 million. He took to the challenge with fervor.

After Derrickson finished writing the script with writing partner Paul Harris Boardman, Dimension Films green-lighted the project (gave it the okay to go into production). Dimension Films head Bob Weinstein was so impressed with the script that he hired Derrickson to direct the unbelievably low-budgeted film. Only months later, Derrickson was in production on the $1.8 million *Hellraiser: Inferno*, at the very least a step up for the dead-end franchise and Scott Derrickson's gory introduction to Hollywood film directing.

"The process on [*Hellraiser*] ended up being really a positive one because they let us write the script the way we wanted it and then Bob Weinstein let me direct the movie. And it was such small movie. They were off shooting *Reindeer Games*, which was a $40 million movie, and *Scream 3* and *Texas Rangers*, which was a big movie for them. They just left me alone, and I never had an executive on the set. It was a tough movie because of how little money we had. With the exception of the budget, I got to make the movie I wanted to make."

At the end of the day, *Hellraiser: Inferno* is, without a doubt, a horror film you watch entirely at your own risk, but the bottom line is that it goes where *Hellraiser* had never gone before—and boldly. To cite a few examples: *Inferno*'s protagonist walks a meaningful character arc from inciting incident to resolution; the plot, while confusing and purposefully erratic, comes to a reasonable conclusion in the final scenes; and the use of the infamous *Hellraiser* demons is as subtle as the genre will permit. On the technical side, the camera movements and lighting are subtle enough to suggest a director with a taste for more sophisticated fare. This kind of sparse filmmaking is rare in the low-budget, B-movie, horror film industry. On top of that, the pseudo-redemptive themes that flicker throughout a few scenes in the movie fully realize themselves in the movie's showdown.

Of course, when discussing a project like this, some questions need to be addressed. For example, how much does someone struggle with making ultra-violent and grotesque films with a debatable message?

"The *Hellrasier* movie I made is an extremely graphic movie about hell," Derrickson admitted. "I mean, it really was an attempt to sort of recreate a new vision of hell itself. That needed to be a very lurid and graphic place. I think there's a tremendous amount of sex and violence and even profanity in the Bible. That in and of itself ought to liberate Christians from feeling paranoid about its use."

As a follower of Jesus dealing with a Christian subculture that is often as oppressive as Hollywood is graphic, a Christian filmmaker has to straddle a scary fence when making this kind of film. It's interesting that Derrickson's comment concerns his personal feeling of peace and not his need to appease the Christian ghetto of which he is a part. But inevitably, Christian or not, the question arises: Is Derrickson compromising his moral or filmic integrity to move ahead in Hollywood? Could this be compared to Francis Ford Coppola, who, after being raised Catholic, got his start in what he called "exploitation films"? Coppola talked about this briefly in a speech he gave in the early '70s.

"I was willing to do anything to get to make more films," Coppola said. "And the best opportunity was in the field of the exploitation film—by which I mean nudie, science fiction, horror, and religious films."[1] At the time, Coppola's peers criticized him because he was willing to compromise just to make movies. But unlike many of Coppola's peers, from his meager beginnings, he went on to direct big films with major artistic and commercial impact on society as a whole. Derrickson, similarly, chose to move into an exploitation film genre to earn his stripes, and yet, did he really compromise?

"I can't say I never had any battles of conscience with it, because I never want to not ask myself those questions," Derrickson said. "But I certainly am quite content with everything I've ever written or shot." Despite potential naysayers, it appears as though he has affected his audience, crafted an interesting story in a genre well known for less than interesting stories, and infiltrated the walls of Hollywood. Now Derrickson has more opportunities than ever to influence large audiences through bigger mainstream film projects.

The most intriguing thing about this franchise has nothing to do with the first four films, but with *Hellraiser: Inferno*, its creator, and what could be perceived as a spiritual paradox utilizing one of Hollywood's most gory creations. But obviously God can redeem anyone or anything that He chooses, even something that many would dismiss as ludicrous. Most curious of all, how can one man coming from a Christian perspective watch these films and find a way to write their sequel? Talk about a fascinating source for a spiritual dilemma. Now, what can other filmmakers and film lovers learn from his experience? Don't rush to a quick decision—there's still a lot of evidence yet to sift through.

PINHEAD

"I'm very happy about the lack of Pinhead in *Inferno*. THE SERIES HAD BECOME A PINHEAD SHOW ... but if I had to do it over again, I'd put a bit more of him in there for the sake of the fans."
—Scott Derrickson

Like Freddy Krueger or Jason Voorhees before him, the demon called Pinhead is an infamous character in the history of horror cinema. At the very least, he is the visually arresting figurehead that is most identified with this series. To see him in one of the *Hellraiser* films, Pinhead is a strange character that could only have been created by pounds of make-up, black leather, plastic props, and masses of eyeliner. He has the pale skin of an albino, dull black eyes like a shark's, and a grid of pins sticking out of his head that are vaguely reminiscent of something spawned by a nail gun.

You may have seen Pinhead on video jackets at the video store or in the previews for one of the films. You might have seen one of these films for yourself, although it wouldn't be surprising if you haven't. Infamous horror writer Clive Barker wrote and directed the original *Hellraiser* film and released it in 1986 to the delight of B-movie consumers everywhere. For unknown reasons, it became an underground phenom-enon. Of the eight *Hellraiser* films made thus far, the majority of them are grisly affairs with farfetched plots, mediocre special effects, and too many death scenes for anyone's taste. Gratuitous violence and gore are some of the standards by which these types of films are judged by their fans. The most effective thrillers are films that create subtext and tension, leave much to the imagination, imply just about everything, and ratchet up the stakes with subtle twists and shades of foreshadowing. Unfor-tunately, both the thriller and horror genres are better known for their bloody shootouts and overt plot twists that lumber toward viewers with all the subtlety of a sledgehammer.

Inferno is a horror movie that cannot escape these leaden elements, but the film aims high, works with the characters as much as the special ef-fects, and dabbles in more subtlety than any of the four previous films. The truth of the matter is that Derrickson is a filmmaker of much more precision than Barker will ever be.

HELLRAISER AS SCREWTAPE

"I was really into *The Screwtape Letters* coming out of graduate school. I had been rereading it, and I was sensing that there was something about that book and its ability to speak to popular culture—and yet it was such a dynamic expression of a very specific faith."
—Scott Derrickson

It's a safe bet that the last thing you'd call to mind in conjunction with *Hellraiser* is a book by a wizened old English theologian named Clive Staples (C.S.) Lewis. The challenge here is to compare two pieces of pop culture that come from completely opposite ends of the spectrum, discuss their differences, and learn something from their similarities. Lewis' most well known book, *The Screwtape Letters*, offers a mischievous and ironic slant on the difficulties and temptations of life as a follower of Christ. Through the pen of a fictional demon named Screwtape, Lewis created what amounts to a satiric demon's guide to winning human souls. The idea was to give people a unique, poignant, and often hilarious view into their own raw humanity. The book immediately caught on around the world, became an international best seller, and is still widely read today.

When Derrickson mentioned that he found inspiration in *The Screwtape Letters* when working on the movie, it seemed like strange company for *Hellraiser: Inferno*, and yet somehow exactly right. The book came up in casual conversation when Derrickson discussed why he liked to work in the horror genre.

"I love the horror genre for how cinematic it is," Derrickson said. "I gravitated, I think initially, toward the horror genre because, of all the genres, I think it is the genre that is most friendly to the subject matter of faith and belief in religion. The more frightening and sort of dark and oppressive a movie is, the more free you are to explore the supernatural and explore faith. The two just somehow go hand-in-hand really nicely. I became very interested in it for that reason, and *The Screwtape Letters* was the beacon."

While Derrickson's film and *The Screwtape Letters* strike similar chords, neither the mainstream media nor the Church came to recognize *Hellraiser: Inferno* as the postmodern version of the book. Nonetheless, the similarities are there.

Obviously, the creators of *Hellraiser* and *The Screwtape Letters* share first names, and it seems as though Barker's Pinhead would fit nicely into the host of oddly named demons in *The Screwtape Letters*, which includes Wormwood, Slumtrimpet, and Glubose.

But even in terms of story and theology, the two aren't dissimilar. The key parallel is found in the idea that a discussion of hell, or from the perspective of hell, implies the existence of heaven and God. Lewis asserts this boldly by leaving God out of the discussion for the most part. When Screwtape mentions God in passing, he refers to Him as the enemy, and he calls Satan "our father below." Derrickson, on the other hand, allows Pinhead to imply the existence of God by default, in the simple fact that he is himself, a demon from hell. Several moments push this a step further, shading Derrickson's depiction of hell with hints of an opposite place or idea of God. In one of the final scenes, Pinhead says to Joseph, the protagonist in *Inferno*, "You have destroyed your own innocence. You are your own king. This is the hell you have created for yourself."[2]

Joseph is a dirty cop who cheated on his wife, does drugs, betrays the loyalty of his partner, lies, steals from a crime scene, and tortures one of his sources during an investigation. Pinhead is right in his analysis, because Joseph has created his own hell in a series of calculated and sinful acts.

He says to Joseph, who happens to be very good at chess, "Who is the king in this game, Joseph? That is the question you must ask yourself."

Joseph responds, "I don't understand."

Pinhead replies coolly, "Ah, the eternal refrain of humanity. Pleading ignorance, begging for mercy. Please, help me, I don't understand. This is the life you chose, Joseph. All the people you hurt, all the appetites you indulge, you have allowed your flesh to consume your spirit."[3] It is interesting to hear a fire and brimstone sermon coming from this character, whose previous rants had been less articulate, less redemptive. While it's awkward to read about this demonic character with these implications in mind, isn't it just as awkward to read about Lewis' Wormwood, Slumtrimpet, and Glubose?

Like the Bible itself, *The Screwtape Letters* is severe in its description of sin and authentic in its definition of humanity and the failings of all people. Whereas Lewis' approach is decidedly more proper, Derrickson portrays the same idea of referring to God simply by implication.

DETERRENCE AND SUBTLETY

"I'M A RECOVERING FUNDAMENTALIST. I think when people break out of that, they break out of that with a vengeance and, hence, the horror films." —Scott Derrickson

When reading *The Screwtape Letters'* description of how demons can tempt humans away from godly things, we realize that this is a warning. Lewis is telling Christians to beware of this kind of temptation or trickery. In the same way, *Hellraiser: Inferno* shows Joseph going through trials of temptation and failing by describing exactly how demons trick or tempt. The tactic at work here is not historical reporting or exploitation, but deterrence, a kind of warning to the audience through experience.

A country avoids war by building up a vast arsenal of weapons to demoralize or put fear into an enemy. Here we find that film does the same thing by being openly graphic about the consequences of various actions. In *Hellraiser: Inferno*, Derrickson shows Joseph sinking to the depths of hell, describes for us the pain and suffering he feels, and then takes a moment to point out that it's his own fault for ending up there.

It's much like the blunt anti-drug commercial that said of an egg, "This is your brain," and of the egg bubbling and popping in a frying pan, "This is your brain on drugs." This kind of deterrence can also be seen in other films like *Trainspotting* or *Requiem for a Dream*, both of which depict the results of drugs in the worst possible ways. The effect of such brutal depictions is arguably one that would deter those in the audience from ever wanting to try drugs or continue using them.

It's true that *Hellraiser: Inferno* depicts a brutal picture of hell, but it also outlines the simple, sinful choices Joseph made to get there. Like *The*

Screwtape Letters, life is shown from another angle. The consequences of a person's actions boldly declare a moral warning to the audience. In a sense, Derrickson is telling every B-movie horror film fan who watches the film, "This is NOT how we should live our lives—take note of it."

Granted, it's a controversial form of persuasion, but if the goal is to allow the audience the opportunity to think about their morality, their faith, or their life, it's probably worth the chance. The very same B-movie film lovers would not be impressed by a sermon about the consequences of hell or the dangers of living a life of overindulgence. But would they pay attention to a horror movie that displays the same message? *Hellraiser: Inferno* reaches its audience, speaking to them in their language. Has the film made a difference in the lives of the audience? Who knows? But filmmakers can learn from the method.

One concept from *The Screwtape Letters* that becomes a major theme of the book is the comparison between the subtleties of evil and spectacular wickedness. Screwtape writes to his nephew Wormwood about how to seduce a Christian away from his faith. In his letters, Screwtape suggests that subtleties of evil are more effective than spectacular acts of wickedness, because they draw less attention and, thus, embed themselves into the lives of humans unnoticed.

In some ways, *Hellraiser: Inferno* is the characterization of this idea. Over the course of the film, Joseph is slowly wrapped up in a series of increasingly sinful activities that mark his eventual downfall. At first, it's almost unnoticeable because he is so intently focused on solving a particular crime. His intense focus distorts his own reality so much that by the time he realizes what he's been doing to himself, it's too late. This is exactly the tactic Screwtape describes for his nephew in winning over Christian souls.

When compared with the halting attempts at portraying spectacular wickedness of its predecessors, *Hellraiser: Inferno* also represents a more subtle approach. What does this say about the series as a whole? Maybe the previous filmmakers ought to have read *The Screwtape Letters* before they called "Action!"

DANTE AND INFERNO

"The *Hellrasier* movie I made is an extremely graphic movie about hell. I MEAN IT REALLY WAS AN ATTEMPT TO SORT OF RE-CREATE a new vision of hell itself." —Scott Derrickson

One thing people fully expect from a horror movie that contains the word "inferno" in the title is a wide array of imagery having to do with fire. But the film doesn't feature a single frame that contains any sort of fiery image, save an early scene where a candle burns in the corner of an otherwise nondescript room.

Oddly, Derrickson and his writing partner seemed to have played down the fire image, perhaps to highlight the title's reference to Dante's classic poem "The Inferno." "The Inferno" is one poem in a trilogy of epic poems that has come to be known as Dante's *The Divine Comedy*. The trilogy of poems deals with heaven, hell, and purgatory and is widely regarded as three of literature's most renowned works.

"The Inferno" is written from the perspective of Dante himself as he tours the various levels of hell. The ancient poet Virgil is Dante's fiction-al guide through the nine circles of hell, where they discover the sins contained in each circle and the punishments reserved for specific types of sinners. Dante's description of hell descends by sin as he passes knolls, cliffs, woods, ditches, pits, and lakes reserved for all types of people including gluttons, heretics, flatterers, fortune-tellers, hypocrites, and thieves, in that order. Of course, many other types of sinners are sighted during the tour through hell. Dante also finds it appropriate to assign judgment to actual figures in history, including former popes, poets, senators, and other leaders, by sighting them in various circles.

Maybe Derrickson chose this title for its imagery and the book's description of hell, something he endeavored to create in the movie. In fact, in the final scenes of *Hellraiser: Inferno*, Joseph runs through a hallway opening doors, where he meets the people he sinned against throughout the movie. The scene is visually startling and seems to draw on Dante's visitation of the different levels and kinds of sin.

Another parallel that may or may not have been intended can be found in the twenty-first canto of Dante's "The Inferno." In lines forty-five through sixty, Dante describes sinners in the eighth circle sunk in boiling pitch, or tar, being guarded by black winged demons. Whenever one of the sinners tries to come out of the pitch, the demons go after him with grappling hooks, which is an image of torture that is utilized to similar effect in the *Hellraiser* movies.

Ultimately, Derrickson's referencing of an iconic literary hallmark for his horror movie is an unheard of nod to ancient literature that gives *Hellraiser: Inferno* that much more depth.

PLAYING THE **DEVIL'S ADVOCATE**

"It may be impossible to make a really good movie about God that people can take seriously. BUT YOU CAN REALLY SPEAK TO THEM BY MAKING A GOOD MOVIE ABOUT THE DEVIL, and therefore inherently making a movie about God." —Scott Derrickson

When seeking to discern the benefits of discussing faith from another angle, *The Screwtape Letters* is the previous century's boldest attempt at playing the devil's advocate. Perhaps Scott Derrickson's foray into discussing faith in a filmic forum is a sign of things to come. If film is truly the new literature, then *Hellraiser* is simply a dime store novel with a subtle theme of redemption. But it's undeniable that the next generation will increasingly use film as their primary form of expression, of literary discourse. It's critical that Christians make themselves a part of that conversation.

This logic makes a lot of sense, especially when looking at the list of other dark movies that tackle issues of faith, including *The Exorcist*, *Lost Souls*, *The Prophecy*, *The Omen*, *Frailty*, and *The Devil's Advocate*. Brian P. Stone, in his book *Faith and Film*, talks about a similar genre—namely, science fiction—as a powerful force in discussing deeper human issues.

"When science fiction first began to appear almost a hundred years ago, it was considered little more than the product of end-of-the-century anxiety," Stone says in a chapter about the film *Contact*. "Since that time, however, it has served as an important avenue for dealing with heavy questions such as the shape of the ultimate reality, the meaning of life, and the place of humans beings in the cosmos. Though religion and religious faith are not always an explicit preoccupation of contemporary film, it is not unusual to find science fiction dealing head-on with issues that have religious importance as an underlying and recurring theme."[4]

So what does this mean for Christian writers, critics, audiences, and aspiring filmmakers? Could it be true that science fiction and horror films carry weightier faith questions than other films? Perhaps this phenomenon can be attributed to these films' special effects, stylish and offbeat characters, and radical plot lines. Either way, the implicit challenge to spiritual filmmakers is not to overlook the B-film genres as a sub par breeding ground for a powerful filmmaking experience.

In Derrickson's experience, "the more frightening and dark and oppressive a movie is, the more free you are to explore the supernatural and explore faith."[5] His point makes sense, especially after watching films like *Bless the Child*, *Stigmata*, *The Third Miracle*, and even the laughable *End of Days*. The theme of darkness and the supernatural element is consistent in each film, but the spiritual discussion seems wide open.

It is especially important for us to remember again that God can use all sorts of spectacular and unpredictable tools to reveal His truth to people. In fact, if our God is capable of using anything and anyone for His will, maybe it's not too much to suggest that God can use horror films for His glory, too.

NOTES:

1. Francis Ford Coppola quoted in Fred Baker with Ross Firestone, *Movie People: At Work in the Business of Film* (Lancer Books, New York: 1973).

2. Scott Derrickson, Paul Harris Boardman, *Hellraiser: Inferno* (Dimension Films, 2000).

3. Ibid.

4. Brian P. Stone, *Faith and Film* (Chalice Press, St. Louis, Missouri: 2000) p. 14–15.

5. Brian Godawa, *Hollywood Worldviews* (InterVarsity Press, Downers Grove, IL: 2002).

DIRECTOR

A Scanner Darkly — 2005
$5.15/Hr. (TV) — 2004
Before Sunset — 2004
The School of Rock — 2003
Live From Shiva's Dance Floor — 2003
Tape — 2001
Waking Life — 2001
The Newton Boys — 1998

SubUrbia — 1996
Before Sunrise — 1995
Dazed and Confused — 1993
Slacker — 1991
It's Impossible to Learn to Plow
by Reading Books — 1988

PRODUCER

A Scanner Darkly — 2005

$5.15/Hr. (TV) — 2004
Before Sunset — 2004
Waking Life — 2001
The Newton Boys — 1998
Before Sunrise — 1995
Dazed and Confused — 1993
Slacker — 1991
It's Impossible to Learn to Plow
by Reading Books — 1988

WRITER

$5.15/Hr. (TV) — 2004
Before Sunset — 2004
Dazed and Confused — 1993
Slacker — 1991
It's Impossible to Learn to Plow
by Reading Books — 1988

08 RICHARD LINKLATER

⊠ THE INDEPENDENT SPIRIT

"There are so many people who gave up on cinema so long ago, and it's sad. I guess I get a sense that the older audience, that over-thirty abstract audience, they'll go to the big hit, but they really don't see movies as nourishment. So you can't blame studio execs for gearing everything to eighteen-to-twenty-four-year-olds, because that's who's buying tickets, and we're in a free market system here." —Richard Linklater

When Richard Linklater makes a movie, he looks for an edge. Every film he's made in fifteen years of writing, directing, and producing is driven by a spirit of innovation, style, and low-budget ingenuity, despite the occasional bigger budget studio hit. For the consistently introspective and restlessly spiritual filmmaker, truth defies definition, and ultimately, God is one of a number of fascinating ideas. Like some of his other indie film contemporaries, Linklater's movies always reflect a deep searching that is punctuated by high-caliber creativity.

In many ways, Linklater is the true postmodern. His movies highlight themes of tolerance for other beliefs, ideas, and philosophies, and in interviews, he is hesitant to indict anyone for his or her ideas about life. In one interview, Linklater talked about his film *Dazed and Confused* and the extensive drug use portrayed as a reflection of teenagers in the 1970s. In the interview, Linklater related drug use, a practice he neither condemns nor recommends, to a spiritual search that everyone fills in different ways.

"It seems that most people have a need to transcend, to find a spiritual quality," Linklater said. "It's just how that gets answered. You can be a Bible-thumper answering that need or a New-Ager. We all find our own rituals and our own methods of answering that spiritual need. You kind of need to plug into some other kind of ideology. It could be any kind of dogmatic thing."[1]

But when asked where Linklater himself finds that kind of spiritual transcendence, he pins his personal devotion on film itself. "Cinema, yeah, that's what I'm plugged into," he said. "It became my view of the whole world, I think. That's my twelve-step program."[2]

For Christian filmmakers looking to tackle Hollywood via the independent film route, know this: Linklater has mastered the key to riveting the eyes and ears of the Hollywood elite—do something that raises eyebrows, be different, and stand out from the crowd through consistent innovation and risk.

In studying 2004's *Before Sunset*, viewers find an introduction to the bold innovation that keeps Linklater on the blinding edge. Both the film and its prequel, *Before Sunrise*, are convention-defying romances that sashay across genre lines with reckless aplomb, following two people through a series of lovers' plights.

Before Sunrise, which was released in 1995, is filled with constant conversation (a Linklater staple) and a few romantic sidelines, such as the musings of an entertaining street poet, an old fortune-teller, and a strange pair of German playwrights.

The film flows organically, holding to no particular formula, instead grappling with the kind of tasteful romantic evening that has befallen people around the world since the beginning of time. Just before the credits roll, the couple parts on a train platform, promising to meet up six months later. *Before Sunrise* is wonderfully free of the typical studio plot strictures, which gives each moment, including the open-ended final moments, an immediacy that's engaging to watch.

The long awaited sequel, which debuted in theaters in the summer of 2004, finds two main characters, Jesse (Ethan Hawke) and Celine (Julie Delpy), meeting for the first time since that morning on the train platform, nine years earlier. The couple strikes up another organic conversation that continues the story by touching on the flourishes and frailties of relationships.

When Linklater was preparing to shoot *Before Sunset*, he decided to up the stakes of his story and shoot the film in real time, something he had only done once before with his 2001 film *Tape*. When a filmmaker makes a movie in real time—and by the way, there aren't many who attempt it—he or she must cut the film to reflect the exact amount of time that passes by onscreen. For example, the time that elapses over the course of the story of *Before Sunset* is approximately eighty minutes. That is also the film's running time; hence, real time. The TV show *24* is a great example of a story also shot in near real time.

But Linklater always drives his innovation with weight and purpose. In *Before Sunset*, Jessie and Celine, meet up after not having seen each other for nine years. This time around, Jesse has to catch a plane in an hour and a half instead of the next day, as with *Before Sunrise*.

"[Real time] gave the film a certain continuity, and most importantly, because of the situation with Jessie having to leave, I thought that that would [create] a natural dramatic tension," Linklater said. "It seems simple, you know, but think about this: The entire film had to work like a play. We couldn't cut out. We were sort of married to all of it. That just necessitated us to work really, really hard in rehearsal. I don't think you can work much harder than Julie and Ethan and I worked on that aspect."

Linklater also experiments in *Before Sunset* with a series of long unbroken shots, following the couple as they walk through a series of Paris neighborhoods. The camera follows them slowly, sometimes winding through tunnels, through gardens, and up or down staircases. Shooting a film like this in real time is a gargantuan technical challenge. The lighting from one scene to the next has to match, when scenes might be shot at completely different times of day.

Before Sunset also tackles a unique kind of romantic comedy that, like its predecessor, is entirely unconventional in its meandering form, unpredictable plot, and open-ended final frames. Both films leave the viewer in midstride with an entirely unresolved conclusion. And unlike just about every Hollywood romance you'll ever see, *Before Sunset* stages scenes of rambling dialogue and static cameras that would send shudders down the spines of studio executives. In one such scene, Jesse and Celine trade intense verbal jabs for one emotionally intense and unbroken eight-minute camera shot that takes place in the back of a European minivan.

In the film's production notes, producer Anne Walker commented on the acting in the scene. "The only reason this movie is possible is because Julie and Ethan are such incredibly talented actors," Walker said. "We filmed an eight-minute scene in the car, and they could just go all the way through from start to finish, without one stop, not missing a beat. I think that's extraordinary."[3]

When it comes to writing the script, Linklater also deviated from the norm. With *Before Sunset*, he asked his primary actors to email him pages of dialogue, ideas about relationships, or monologues that might come from the main characters. After formulating their dialogue and his own into a workable script, Linklater rehearsed the actors for two weeks, changing lines to suit his actors' conversational styles.

"I always thought the first script was the architecture, and the second script that I would come up with, with the actors, would be the essence," Linklater said. "Actors to varying degrees want to collaborate on the material. Ethan and Julie—they are both writers, they've both made films, they're very smart people."

Working this way obviously has its risks, but Linklater hasn't skipped a beat since launching his career in 1991 with the Sundance Film Festival's off-kilter hit *Slacker*. During an interview to promote *Before Sunset*, Linklater confided that his original script for *Before Sunrise* wouldn't have worked. "If we would have done that script word-for-word thinking it was any good, it would have been a big failure," Linklater said. "The actors had to give a layer of themselves." The secret? Linklater rehearses his actors relentlessly, using that time to change dialogue and to allow an actor to sink into his or her character. "The goal [with *Before Sunset*] was just to make it seem like we turned on the camera," Linklater said. "It was, ultimately, a very rehearsal-intense process."

And the innovative spirit Linklater embodies is attractive to those who work with him. "Doing something that feels like it's a little outside the normal terrain is thrilling because you might fall flat on your face," Hawke said, commenting on Linklater's style in *Before Sunset*'s production notes. "But if it works, it'll also be kind of unique, which is a good life's goal if you're involved in the arts at all, to try to find your own voice. I think people telling stories makes you feel not alone in the universe."[4]

THE **HISTORY** OF RICHARD LINKLATER

"I think there are two kinds of filmmakers—ONES THAT HAD THEIR LITTLE 8 MM CAMERAS and their trains and were setting fires and blowing them up and crashing into each other, and then there're the

ONES WHO READ A LOT and were going to the theater and maybe reading philosophy." —Richard Linklater[5]

For fans of independent cinema, Richard Linklater is a household name. The innovative writer, director, and producer has been toughing it out in the pseudo-Hollywood trenches (otherwise known as Austin, Texas) for years, like other Texan filmmakers Quentin Tarantino, Guillermo del Toro, Robert Rodriguez, and Tim McCanlies. Not only that, Linklater lit the kindling that has made Austin one of the film industry's most vibrant hotspots outside of Hollywood. Even before he was making radical movies, Linklater was aggressively promoting independent films.

In 1985, he founded the Austin Film Society (AFS), which was incorporated as a nonprofit educational organization in 1986. The statement on the bottom of the society's website reads, "The Austin Film Society promotes the appreciation of film and supports creative filmmaking."[6] Since 1986, the AFS has offered a number of vital filmmaking programs, including providing grants to young, emerging filmmakers (over $400,000 to more than one hundred and forty projects); presenting screenings of little-seen independent and foreign films; bringing in visiting filmmakers to speak; showcasing the work of local filmmakers; holding various filmmaking workshops; and publishing a bimonthly newsletter.

In the year 2000, the AFS created the one-stop filmmakers' paradise known as Austin Studios, in partnership with the city of Austin. According to the AFS website, Austin Studios, which is housed in five former airplane hangers, features ten thousand square feet of production office space and more than one hundred thousand square feet of production space. Austin Studios has been host to numerous film projects since its opening, including *Secondhand Lions*, *Spy Kids 3*, *The Rookie*, *The 25th Hour* and many others.

After his film society began to gather a large local following of devout film lovers, Linklater started making his own films. The first feature he made is the awkwardly titled *It's Impossible to Learn to Plow by Reading Books*, which he shot on Super 8 mm film in 1988.

In 1991, Linklater made the breakout hit *Slacker,* a movie that should have failed. It follows one hundred different characters over a single twenty-four-hour period. Roger Ebert likened the film to "a cue ball with a camera."[7] But the film works and was nominated for the Grand Jury Prize at the 1991 Sundance Film Festival and garnered an Independent Spirit Award nomination as well.

"I think I got really lucky with *Slacker,*" Linklater told an interviewer. "That was a film that probably shouldn't have been seen. That was such an underground work, from the margins. I am still amazed to this day [because] ... I thought I was making something that would alienate everyone in a certain way, just the structure of it, there's no story."[8]

Soon after *Slacker,* Linklater dove into a variety of projects, trading studio films for independently financed films seemingly at whim. After his first studio film, the '70s high school film *Dazed and Confused*, which nostalgically captures the essence of a drug-induced high school blur, Linklater tackled his own unique version of a romantic comedy with the refreshingly open-ended *Before Sunrise.*

Then Linklater helmed another slacker flick in *SurUrbia,* a movie that portrays a view of teenage America that is unabashedly pessimistic with a dash of social commentary. The film follows a group of young people who hang out in a convenience-store parking lot, trading ideas about the ugliness of America that seem to stem from Linklater's own thoughts on the subject. He has talked extensively about his disillusionment with success and his ultimately nonconformist views.

"I always sensed instinctively from the earliest age that I was being lied to," Linklater told interviewer David Walsh. "In school, the teachers, the principal, whatever system was in place ... The biggest lie about America is, 'Well, it's not perfect, but it's the best we've ever come up with.' That's just drilled into your head from the first grade on ... I think this bloated thing is going to come crashing down."[9]

Linklater tackled his second studio project in what was his most conventional film to date. The bank robber story *The Newton Boys*, which released in theaters in 1998, starred Matthew McConaughey, Vincent D'Onofrio, Skeet Ulrich, and Ethan Hawke. The film charts the true story of four poverty stricken brothers who were sharecroppers in the 1920s. After a stint in jail, the oldest brother Willis convinces his three brothers to help him rob banks to fight back and avoid a life of extreme poverty. Later, after the brothers gain a reputation around the country, they pull off one of the most infamous train robberies in American history.

"[Willis] was kind of a genius criminal, although he was uneducated," Linklater said. "He had an extraordinary mind, a restless mind. Anyway, when I found this story, I was really taken with it. You're talking about outsiders in society and how they deal with it and how they justify what they do. I can relate to that."[10]

In 2001, Linklater unleashed a powerful duo of groundbreaking movies with the neurotically animated postmodern mindbender *Waking Life* and the gripping *Tape*, which was shot in one room and in real time. Both movies are compelling, but it is the fascinating *Waking Life* in which Linklater tackles the subject of God, self, daydreaming, and a whole list of random and loosely associated ideas that bombard the viewer for two hours.

WAKING **LIFE**

"[*Waking Life*] was just a film of ideas; I couldn't do that every time. IT'S KIND OF A KITCHEN-SINK MOVIE. A lot of scenes I had dropped from other movies in the past I could include here." —Richard Linklater

Linklater is clearly a filmmaker who loves ideas, although he never settles on his own definition of truth. Whatever Linklater's beliefs, the visual tapestry of the digitally-shot-then-animated film that is *Waking Life* presents some very interesting ideas about identity and God. In this film, Linklater continues his devotion to the abstract by going one step further than *Slacker* in exploring ideas, philosophy, and film format.

Waking Life follows one young man on his attempt to escape an animated dream world filled with talky characters, fluctuating landscapes, and fluid discussions. The film plays like a series of choppy lectures and stream-of-consciousness rants that bring our nameless main character to the realization that he's dreaming, though he can't seem to wake up.

The film's animated form is slightly jarring at first, as characters walk through a colorful, undulating landscape. Linklater filmed each scene on a digital camera and then drew on the talents of Bob Sabiston, who animated the characters and the environment on top of the digitally shot version of the film. The form of the movie is an apt representation of its story, the dream world.

Critics have hazarded guesses about the film's overall meaning, despite the lack of true continuity. Some have said the film is about Linklater's fondness for daydreaming, while others called it a radical visualization of self-awareness and identity.

"Daydreaming is a productive activity," Linklater said in one interview. "Where do you get your ideas from? If you're working all day, that kind of kills a lot. It's also about visualizing your ideal world, both the kind of world you live in and also who you want to hang around with and what you want to spend your time doing, what are your ideal physical circumstances."[11]

Linklater riffed on self-awareness in another interview: "This whole movie's such a journey, he's traveling in his mind, and everything he meets is helping him become more aware. If you're human, you don't even have any choice," he said. In response to a question about choice, he said, "Free will, that's a good one, that's right up here with God. These are really fundamental questions you ask yourself at an early age, but you never really answer them, you just circle around to it again."[12]

In interviews, Linklater often returns to the ideas of daydreaming (an idea often called Linklater's dominant theme), self-awareness, identity, and the nature of reality when discussing *Waking Life*. Fundamentally, the film tackles more subjects than is possible to contemplate in any short space. As a result, *Waking Life* is a conversation on the surface, a formula-bucking ode to ideas that moves so quickly through a textbook full of life discussions that none of them sticks totally. The overall goal of the film is the experience, while the ideas themselves are not.

One scene stands out in the midst of the film's metaphor and allusion. It's a scene titled, "The Holy Moment." In this scene, two unidentified men sit at a table discussing film theory. The man doing the majority of the talking starts to discuss the French film theorist Andre Bazin, which turns out the following monologue: "For [Bazin], reality and God are the same. And so what film is really capturing is like, God incarnate, creating, you know, like this very moment, God is manifesting as this. So film is a record of God or the face of God or the ever-changing face of God."[13]

This short monologue can be construed in any number of ways, from a naturalistic worldview to a biblical one, but following this exchange, the two men decide to stage a "holy moment." Immediately, they stop and look at each other, hoping to experience something holy, a connection of some sort. The silence lasts a good amount of time, as the men study and stare at each other.

"That truly was something I had never done before, that particular scene," Linklater said. "You know, I say I'm always so rehearsal intensive. That was one of the only scenes in my whole ten-year film career that I kind of let the camera roll. But I knew something was coming. And the holy moment was a totally spontaneous moment—I didn't know that was coming. I was just wondering as I was filming, *How is this gonna to end?*"

Linklater said he let the camera roll on his two actors for more than thirty seconds, as the two men improvised the scene and sought out their holy moment. As the scene fades out, the two men slowly morph into clouds and sky, another animator's luxury that Linklater tapped for all it was worth.

"That was just unfolding in front of me," Linklater said. "And at the time, you almost don't even totally appreciate it. I mean, it was only in the editing room, because we filmed another thing that I thought would be the scene. We did two different scenes. Then I looked at that in the editing room and I'm like, 'Okay, that's it—we've got to do the Holy Moment.' It's such a great moment."

The short exchange is an example of the spiritual searching—albeit entirely open-ended and lacking in definition—that has become commonplace in Hollywood and in culture. These days, filmmakers themselves are exploring these questions without answering them, leaving only more questions. There is a vast difference between movies that provide an audience with answers—or try to—in a world where relativism is very nearly accepted practice, and movies that ask the right questions, so that the audience can come up with the answers on their own.

The suggestion here is not that relativism should be the Christian standard, thereby foregoing absolute truth, but that Christians direct non-Christian viewers to ask questions and then find the truth on their own. Providing concrete answers in a film implies that the filmmaker is somehow an expert with hard evidence, an assertion that audiences naturally treat with a large amount of incredulity. Filmmakers should not be in the practice of throwing out complexity in favor of "dumbing down" their movies to bring forth a message. But if audience members can be inspired to search for truth themselves, now there's a goal for Christians to aspire to!

In one of *Waking Life*'s final scenes, the young man comes across a man playing pinball, played by Linklater himself. At this point, the young man is flabbergasted, having tried to wake from his dream numerous times. But the pinball player seems to have some answers for him that, for better or for worse, wrap up the film.

"All of life is an eternity," the pinball player says. "All of life is an instant, right now, and we're here, and God is waiting for us to give in. But we keep saying 'no.' All our lives are an eternity of instances where we say 'no thank you.' Until we say 'yes,' and give in and go to heaven."[14]

For those who are curious, Linklater doesn't believe in God—at least, not yet. "My criteria [on *Waking Life*] wasn't truth-based; it was more idea-based, like, is this interesting?" Linklater said. "Like the way I view a lot of things. I don't think many things are like 'true,' whatever that is, but [I wonder], is it interesting enough to toss on my scrap heap?"

Notes

1. Carla Sinclair, John Lebkowsky and Doug Rushkoff, "Slacking in the Seventies," *The GenX Reader* (Ballantine Books, 1994) *www.flank.com/sites/netchick/Lounge/Bookcase/linklater.html* (accessed April 18, 2004).

2. Ibid.

3. Production Notes, *Before Sunset*, Warner Independent Pictures.

4. Ibid.

5. Tim Rhys, "Interview: Richard Linklater," *MovieMaker Magazine*, Issue #30, September 1998, n.p.

6. *www.austinfilmsociety.com*

7. Roger Ebert, "Slacker," *Chicago-Sun Times*, August 23, 1991. *www.suntimes.com/ebert/ebert_reviews/1991/08/666670.html* (accessed June 21, 2004).

8. David Walsh, "You Can't Hold Back the Human Spirit: An Interview with Richard Linklater," *World Socialist* website, March 27, 1998. *www.wsws.org/arts/1998/mar1998/link-m27.shtml* (accessed April 2, 2004).

9. Ibid.

10. Ibid.

11. "Richard Linklater Interview," *Idler*, September 6, 1994, *www.idler.co.uk/html/interviews/interview6.htm* (accessed April 18, 2004).

12. Cynthia Fuchs, "Some Bigger Communication: An Interview with Richard Linklater, *Waking Life*," *www.morphizm.com/recommends/interviews/linklater_waking.html* (accessed April 18, 2004).

13. Richard Linklater, *Waking Life* (Twentieth Century Fox Home Video, 2002).

14. Ibid.

HOLLYWOOD project
FILMOGRAPHY

WRITER

Little House on the Prairie (TV) — 2004
Rebels — 2003
To End All Wars — 2001
The Dream Center:
Hope for the Inner City — 1999
Beyond Paradise — 1998

PRODUCER

To End All Wars — 2001
The Dream Center:
Hope for the Inner City — 1999
Beyond Paradise — 1998

DIRECTOR

Beyond Paradise — 1998

HOLLYWOOD project
FILMOGRAPHY

"It's a daily struggle, because you get up, and you're dealing with jaded, cynical people that have—out of their own self-protection—developed this thick skin. I just know that I'll be useless the moment that happens."
—David L. Cunningham

David L. Cunningham is descended from a long line of ministers, where for seven generations on one side and four generations on the other side, the men of his family have worked in the traditional pulpit. His father Loren Cunningham founded Youth With a Mission (YWAM) more than forty years ago, and David is one of the only men in his family not to pursue a conventional career as a pastor or minister. But the younger Cunningham considers his career a ministry just the same.

"Growing up in the organization of WYAM and having this heritage of ministers, I've been working hard at trying to apply that to this new grid of filmmaking," Cunningham said from Canada, where he was in production on his latest project, the made-for-TV miniseries, *Little House on the Prairie.* "I've been doing this now for about twelve years, and it's just been in the last year or so that it started to kind of dawn on me. I think I've had levels of success at taking a story and putting it into film. In terms of trying to get the bigger picture strategy of, 'How do we transform through filmmaking?' I'm finally starting to understand what that looks like."

Finding that balance in the competitive and often ruthless industry that Hollywood can be isn't an easy task to take on. Cunningham is frank about the challenges he has faced in Hollywood and about the challenges others can expect to face if they decide to make a career out of making movies.

The most refreshing things about Cunningham's story are his drive to succeed, his desire to influence and transform culture, and the innovative lengths to which he has gone, both to represent his faith to the industry and to make movies that declare bold messages in the midst of powerful, moving stories.

"There was a film that had a tremendous impact on me when I first started film school, and that was Ingmar Bergman's *The Seventh Seal,*" Cunningham said. "[It was] the journey of this knight who is battling death during the time of the Crusades, and it's a pretty heady film. But I saw how you could tell a story with significant messages interweaved in it. This filmmaker, he had an agenda, and whether I agreed with his agenda or not really isn't the point. With your life as a filmmaker, somebody who, dare I say, is an artist and a craftsman, I think there's an obligation to use that and be as bold as possible."

This philosophy of making a movie with a powerful story interwoven harmoniously with a redemptive message is often the goal of many Christian filmmakers looking to transform lives through the movies. But the task is so daunting and fraught with narrative pitfalls that often these filmmakers fail in their attempts. Cunningham, on the other hand, has succeeded, in more ways than one, in straddling the scary chasm that exists between ministry and the movie industry.

His 2001 film *To End All Wars* is perhaps one of the twenty-first century's most powerful looks at war and forgiveness and the gray complexities in between. The movie saw a wide release in theaters around the world with international distributors, but sat on a shelf for two years waiting for a North American release as distribution deals were repeatedly struck and dissolved. The film finally released on DVD in June of 2004.

The World War II film, starring Kiefer Sutherland and the Scottish spitfire-of-an-actor, Robert Carlyle, follows Scottish and American soldiers in a Japanese prisoner of war camp. Cunningham's sophomore feature film takes a gritty and unflinching look at the atrocities of war and the forgiveness that can be found in the midst of it. The small but tight-knit group of soldiers who form the film's collective protagonist fight against their captors at first and then eventually learn to forgive them and treat them with honor despite the fact that no honor is extended to them.

The message that rides beneath the story of this film runs contrary to the themes of revenge, vigilantism, and eye-for-an-eye justice that are prevalent in American film and television shows. But it is the themes of forgiveness, compassion, and turning the other cheek that drive the engine of this movie.

To End All Wars represents another very important example of how a filmmaker can bring forth a significant message while maintaining the power and vitality of the story. While earlier in the book, the point was made that the story must be the primary tool in any filmmaker's arsenal, Cunningham demonstrates that a message can exist in harmony with a film's story, not unlike *The Seventh Seal*, the film he studied in college.

In looking at the rest of Cunningham's career, one sees a colorful tapestry of stories about perseverance, creativity, faith, "bulldog tenacity," and ultimately, stories about making movies.

THE **JOURNEY** THERE

"Essentially, there's this kind of a sense from believers in the film industry where you work, and then you go to church or whatever. You get a job and make your way up the chain, and MAYBE YOU CAN HAVE SOME IMPACT—WHICH IS GOOD, don't get me wrong—but I want it to be about a revolution, right?"
—David L. Cunningham

After growing up in YWAM and being around ministry and missionaries his whole life, Cunningham launched into one of YWAM's Discipleship Training Schools (DTS) right out of high school.

A DTS takes young recruits through six months of intensive teaching and outreach, focusing on evangelism and often occurring in two phases: The first twelve-week phase of the DTS takes place in the classroom, and the second twelve-week phase is all about hands-on ministry and outreach.

After Cunningham completed his DTS, he entered a three-month short film course offered by the University of the Nations, literally a global school run by YWAM in over three hundred locations and in more than one hundred and ten different nations around the world. The program opened Cunningham's eyes to film and changed his life forever.

"As soon as I picked up the camera, it was just totally confirmed that this was what I needed to be doing," he said. "From there I got into documentaries and adventure shows and then eventually transferred to USC, where I studied film there for three and a half years. I ended up going to a couple different film schools, just getting equipped."

Before USC, Cunningham went to Vanguard University of Southern California for a year and a half, taking all the film courses they offered, after which he applied and was accepted into USC's highly reputable film production program. After three and a half years, he moved onward again, ultimately graduating from the University of the Nations.

"When we had filmmakers come to the film schools that I was attending, and we had some pretty significant ones coming, I always would ask them, 'What is your philosophical agenda? Why are you making movies?'" Cunningham said. "Almost every time, [the answer] was, 'To entertain. I like to make people laugh; I like to make people cry.' And I was always disappointed with that answer. I was hoping that people had some kind of reason beyond that."

During that time, Cunningham made an effort to study those filmmakers who were actually trying to say something—filmmakers like Oliver Stone and Spike Lee—and he started to pay close attention to how they made a point in the midst of an intriguing story.

All of this was in preparation for his own career, as he geared up to make a statement to the world. While still in film school, Cunningham struck out on his own and started a video production company called Pray For Rain Pictures.

"I started a production company while in film school, out of our dorm room closet," he said. "We put all of our clothes in a box and put an editing suite in there and started doing wedding videos and training videos and karaoke videos. We eventually elevated up to documentaries and more legitimate stuff. By the time I graduated from film school, we had a staff of about eight or nine people and kind of were off and running."

After doing a number of video projects with his business, Cunningham made sure he wasted no time getting started on his first feature film project. So he partnered with his wife to produce his first film and raised almost a million dollars in the process. The funds he raised would be enough to make his low-budget independent feature film debut. "I'd done a lot of documentaries, music videos, training videos, corporate stuff, a whole bunch of things, and our little business was doing pretty good, but I really felt I was supposed to be making movies," Cunningham said of his decision to tackle his first feature. "And no one will really recognize you as a filmmaker until you've made a film."

When he started working on *Beyond Paradise*, Cunningham didn't realize it, but he was about to go to film school all over again. He worked on nearly every aspect of *Beyond Paradise* from concept to theater screen—he co-wrote the script, gathered the financing, produced and directed the film, helped edit it, sent it to film festivals, and self-distributed the film to select theaters; and then, he even saw it do well in a niche market.

The movie wasn't a massive hit, nor was it a film that Cunningham says represents his best work, but it taught the filmmaker more than just filmmaking—it taught him perseverance. After he had the film playing in theaters in Hawaii and other parts of the United States, distributors began to take notice. Then the first-time director finally landed a distribution deal for his little film after his direct-to-theater marketing met with modest success.

"I went out there and raised the money for it," Cunningham said. "I got twenty-seven investors from six countries and all in little chunks of money. I put together a budget and made a movie. It was a two-year process of learning how to make a movie, how to raise the funds and distribute and all the rest. Distribution is incredibly competitive. As of a few years ago, there's about four thousand movies made a year in North America, and only about four hundred of those hit the theaters at a theater near you. The vast majority you never hear of."

The movie itself depicted a picture of Hawaiian culture that people don't see or often want to acknowledge even exists, highlighting the issues of violence, domestic abuse, drug abuse, and prejudice that exist (like anywhere), despite Hawaii's identity as a major tourist spot. The story focuses on a young white man who moved to Hawaii from California only to be surprised by the radical anti-white prejudice that exists in the midst of the island culture. The film juxtaposes the issues faced by teens and the culture at large with the flashy vacationers' reputation the islands have gained.

Soon after *Beyond Paradise* made it to theaters, a producer by the name of Jack Hafer approached Cunningham with another idea for a film. Hafer owned the rights to a book called *To End All Wars*, written by World War II veteran Ernest Gordon, and he also had a rough version of the script by author and screenwriter Brian Godawa. Cunningham said he would take a look at both, and before he knew it, he was off and running on the film project that would take his career to a whole new level.

TO END ALL WARS

"I WAS ABOUT TO GET INTO SOMETHING ELSE, and I didn't think [*To End All Wars*] was what I was supposed to be doing. Then I read the book and a rough draft of the script and felt very strongly that I was supposed to make the thing." —David L. Cunningham

As difficult a journey as *Beyond Paradise* was, *To End All Wars* would test Cunningham's commitment to his chosen profession even more. From the outset, the director knew he had to take this movie to another level all together, but that jump wouldn't be easy. First off, the story, despite its power, was too abrasive for any studio to take on, meaning that yet again, Cunningham, along with Hafer, would have to raise the money themselves.

So when he agreed to direct *To End All Wars*, Cunningham said he gave Hafer his conditions. "Essentially I told Jack, 'Listen, I'll do this, but I think we're going to have to do what I did,'" Cunningham said. "'We're going to have to go out and raise the money.' I said, 'I've got three conditions. One is that we make it independently, that we do it right away, and that we make it in my home state of Hawaii, because I have developed the infrastructure there and the relationships to be able to pull the favors I need.' So he said, 'Yeah, let's go.'"

The two men dove in immediately and started to talk up the project, raising money right and left. They immediately sought out Cunningham's primary investor from *Beyond Paradise* and then many others, raising nearly $11 million over the course of the project. Although it may sound easy, the simple truth of the matter is that it wasn't.

The film was only weeks away from going into production when the stock market took a major hit. They had already raised the majority of the money, finalized the script, lined up a crew, and were in the process of signing on the cast. Suddenly, some of the project's major investors had lost a big part of their investment money, and half the money Hafer and Cunningham had raised for the film was gone, just like that. This began a sequence of events that wound up being a daily faith journey that would test Cunningham and Hafer each day of the shoot.

When the stock market dropped, the project had just started to gain momentum. Cunningham had flown up to Scotland and pitched the project to critically acclaimed character actor Robert Carlyle, who is well-known for his passionate turns in *The Full Monty*, *Trainspotting*, *Angela's Ashes*, and *The Beach*, and he also played Adolf Hitler in the TV movie *Hitler: The Rise of Evil*. Carlyle agreed to join the cast. The producers also lined up a talented group of American, British, and Scottish actors, including Ciarán McMenamin, who centers the film with a steely performance, and Kiefer Sutherland, who plays the shady, resourceful American in the prison camp.

When asked to explain how they managed to keep their film on track after losing more than half their intended budget, Cunningham offered a warning before telling the rest of the story. "I don't recommend any of this," he said, laughing. "It's a don't-try-this-at-home kind of thing. I'll tell you about it and show you what we did, but you're on your own.

"So we had all that stuff lining up, and we decided we were going to continue to make the movie," Cunningham continued. "We had enough just to get going and to pay the actors. So we didn't tell anybody, but essentially, we were having to raise $500,000 a week to keep the film on schedule and on budget. So I'd call [Hafer] on the way to the set every day and say, 'Do we have enough to make it today?' [He'd say,] 'Yeah. Keep going.'"

On the first day of the movie's production, three people had to be rushed to the hospital (they were fine) but the ambulance ended up making regular trips to the set. Despite the difficulty of the journey, the actors reported that something was different on this film. Robert Carlyle grew so close with the others in the cast that he and six others went out to get matching tattoos to commemorate their experience.

"It was just a massive battle the entire time, and every show is," Cunningham said. "But on this one, there was something really going on. But the actors and the crew sensed that we were doing something special. Kiefer said that this was one of the most significant films he's ever worked on. Something big was going on."

After struggling through an exhausting production, Cunningham was able to shoot the entire film and get all the footage he needed just before they ran out of money. And as most filmmakers know, that's just the beginning of the journey.

Once the team started editing the movie, they continued to go out and raise money to pay for a myriad of postproduction costs that can and do accumulate very quickly. Finally, a British film company called Gold Crest, known for films like *Ghandi* and *The Killing Fields*, stepped in and saved the movie and in exchange, picked up international distribution rights in all but North America.

"They thought the film came into their library quite well, so they moved us to London, and we finished the film there with the London

Symphony Orchestra and posted in their facilities there in SoHo," Cunningham said. "So it's been in distribution outside of the U.S. for almost two years on both theatrical, DVD, and now television."

After selling off international distribution rights, the team set its sights on the bigger step, which was to get the film distributed in the critical North American markets. The film premiered in the United States at the Telluride Film Festival in Colorado, and in Canada at the Toronto Film Festival, both of which are world-renowned. The typical goal at film festivals like these is to build a significant buzz around the movie so the studios will notice it and ultimately buy it. The strategy worked well, and as soon as people began to see the film, the buzz began to build.

Meanwhile, *To End All Wars* also found its way to other festivals, such as the Nashville Film Festival and the Hawaii Film Festival, and in addition, won the Grand Prize, Best Picture, and Crystal Heart Award at the Heartland Film Festival. The Veterans of Foreign Wars also awarded the film its Commander in Chief Medal of Service, Honor, and Pride.

"The film was getting a lot of attention, and Keifer's star was starting to make a big splash with *24*," Cunningham said. "Kiefer was a big supporter of the film, flying around and supporting this thing. We were in some of the most significant film festivals there are, very difficult ones to get into, and we were kind of like headliners and getting critical support."

Finally, when the film landed that coveted distribution deal in North America, the company distributing it went bankrupt. Clearly, Cunningham was frustrated, but he and Hafer tried again and signed another deal with another company ... and then that company eventually fell apart.

"We had like three things in a row, over a year and a half, happen that continued to stall out the North American release of the film," Cunningham said. "It's been very frustrating, because we had so much momentum and good things going for it, and these out of the blue things would happen. Or we had these legitimate people behind the film, and one thing or another would happen. We'd just scratch our heads and say, 'Well, that was weird, let's move on.' We've got this great movie with a great cast, relevant times, and dealing with war. We have this kind of underground fan club who are like angry at us for not having it out.

"Essentially, we ended up getting a deal with Twentieth Century Fox, and it was five months of negotiation. It was just bureaucracy and craziness. Anyways, the story is not over yet with that film."

In the midst of all the frustration over the distribution fiasco, Cunningham began to get loads of attention as a director. Out of the attention came agents, lawyers, and managers, and he began to pick and choose whom he would work with in the future. Most importantly, he began to take numerous meetings for future projects with major Hollywood studios.

"I immediately started getting offers for some other shows as a filmmaker," he said. "Within a short period of time, suddenly I was on the studio map, and they were rushing me around from one studio to the next. It was exciting, but very surreal and disconcerting at the same time."

Due to the underground success of *To End All Wars*, Cunningham signed on to direct a movie for Disney called *Ghost Soldiers* with Gary Sinise. The film made it into production, but was shut down due to an in-house political debate over another project being developed by Miramax, a company Disney owned. Cunningham later agreed to direct Disney's TV miniseries *Little House on the Prairie*, which is set to air on ABC in late 2004.

Whether *To End All Wars* makes any waves in the North American market is yet to be seen, but the film made waves for Cunningham, Hafer, and their cast and crew. It also received kudos from critics like Michael Medved and Eric Metaxas, while Larry King said, "This is a noble story of courage and fortitude that needed to be told."[1]

Impressively, Cunningham gets more ambitious with each consecutive project. And he's not slowing down yet. "I can tell you what's on my burners right now," Cunningham said. "I have an afterlife thriller that takes place in the tunnels of Moscow that I think will be next. I've also got a project set up at Universal on the civil war of Hawaii. I've got a western that I'm also attached to, a kind of gritty western. I've got another project with Brian [Godawa] that we've done together on the civil war of Jerusalem in A.D. 70. So I got quite a few things going and few more. You just never know which one's gonna happen until you're actually on the set making it."

FILM AND MINISTRY

"I think it's time now. I think there's many believers that are in the industry that have kind of come of age, either in their own faith or in their own craft as filmmakers. I THINK IT'S NOW TIME FOR US TO STAND UP AND BE BOLD. I think that the marketplace, the audience, the people out there are ready."—David L. Cunningham

Cuningham is straightforward when answering the question he so often asked of others in film school, "Why do you make movies?" "I believe that I'm called to two areas in the film industry: *to* it, meaning the people that are working within it, that I could be an influence on their lives and transform them; and *through* it," Cunningham said. "The through it part is the audience and the medium of film. Through storytelling, hopefully rock them, inspire them, challenge them, whatever it may take, to in some way get them closer to an understanding of why they are on this planet. So if I had a little mission statement for myself, it would be, 'to it and through it.' To the film industry and through it."

When it comes to ministering to the film industry, Cunningham has carved out his own niche. Typically, filmmakers live out their faith with integrity hoping that it will speak to someone as they work alongside him or her, but Cunningham wasn't content to confine his ministry this way. In a move that paired his beliefs with his on-set needs, he partnered with University of the Nations to bring young, hard-working Christian interns onto his movie shoots to help bring his projects to the screen.

On his latest shoot, the ABC TV mini-series *Little House on the Prairie*, Cunningham was able to bring ten interns with him to assist him on-set. The interns must raise their own support, have a deeply rooted commitment to working in film, and then treat the on-set mission field as a job.

"Right now I've got about ten interns from the University of the Nations that I was able to get onto this film," Cunningham said. "They're all believers, and they're all paying their own way to get here, and there's a process to get on the set. Essentially, I've asked them, 'I'm not asking you to come here to proselytize; I'm asking you to come here and work very hard. If you find an opportunity to share your faith, take it, do it.' I'm wanting them to learn, so they can grow as filmmakers, but I'm also wanting them to season others along the way."

In addition to his on-set intern/missionaries, Cunningham and his team send out regular prayer emails to friends and missionaries around the world. The prayer updates contain requests for everything from good weather to the needs of the interns, the relationships Cunningham has with his producer and editor to specific people on the cast and crew with whom the interns have forged relationships.

Cunningham also tries to minister through his chosen profession by lecturing at film schools and film festivals, including University of the Nations campuses around the world. He has taught at the University of the Nations film program nearly every year since the mid-'90s and even founded a second University of the Nations film program in Switzerland. As his experience has grown, he has also helped facilitate program speakers and the curriculum for the school.

"I'm just a big friend and fan of the school and alumnus of [the program]," Cunningham said. "It's called the school of digital filmmaking, and it's an intensive three-month course and then a three-month internship. And they just started an advanced school, as well as the school for acting for screen. It's interesting what's happening in Kona right now."

For lovers of film and students who desire to join the program in Kona, it takes quite a commitment both to ministry and film to complete it. First, all students must finish a YWAM DTS before they can be even apply to the film program.

If students are eventually admitted to the film school, they will then go through a program that Cunningham calls a "working model," as opposed to a classroom model. The intensive training happens hands-on and, upon graduation, places graduates in internships in which they can actually work in the film business. Cunningham and his film projects are one of the film school's internship resources.

"There's a working model that is still developing, but it's exciting because I think it is the future," Cunningham said. "As believers, we're trained to kind of say, 'Okay, good luck,' and you pat them on the back. 'Here's your diploma.' But they've placed people at Paramount and placed people all over the place."

And though Cunningham is one of the outlets for interns, he is wary of taking on students who aren't fully committed to working in the film business. "I really want people to go through some kind of filtering system, through their own gauntlet, so that I can see that they are worth investing in," he said. "Are they going to make it? And then once they are, I will do anything to help them. Essentially what they need to do is they need to contact University of the Nations."

ACCEPTING THE CALL TO HOLLYWOOD IS NOT EASY

"I'd just be praying, 'GOD, DO NOT LET ME GET CYNICAL, do not let me get cynical,' because I knew the moment I became jaded and cynical was the moment that I would lose touch with my God. And it's a daily struggle, man. It's a daily struggle." —David L. Cunningham

Working in Hollywood is not as glamorous as it's made out to be, and Cunningham has experienced this firsthand. After *To End All Wars* started to turn heads at several renowned film festivals and a few accolades started rolling in, Cunningham began to experience the exhilarating and scary thrill of being courted by the Hollywood elite.

He quickly signed with CAA, one of the most notable agencies in Hollywood, and also partnered with a lawyer shared by Steven Spielberg. He began to take meetings at the studios regularly, looking out for the next project to suit his styles and tastes. All seemed well.

In the midst of all this, Cunningham signed on to direct two studio projects that were later shelved for one reason or another. Despite all the stress and politics, he pushed forward and took the time to write his own script, a film he actually hopes to shoot soon. Then, after weighing all his options, he chose to helm the *Little House on the Prairie* mini-series, which he was filming during the interview, because he wanted to make something his kids could watch.

"I'm in the middle of a very long show right now, and every day, I've got to get up, and I have to deal with bureaucracy and politics," he said. "How, as a believer, am I going to direct today? Not just be inspired, but also handle everything that comes my way? How can I keep the clout I need to get this film made, and get it made right? But also perform in such a way that is honorable to the person that I'm most accountable to?"

Cunningham has also seen how competitive the film industry can be. "On a daily basis, thousands of people are pouring out of film schools and knocking on Hollywood's doors and trying to get going," Cunningham said. "And they are willing to do whatever it takes, whatever it takes. As believers, we need to be as radical, and sometimes it's going to take longer for us to get there, because we're not willing to compromise in certain areas. I would first ask a very big question: 'Why? Why do you feel like you're supposed to be in film?' and, 'Are you sure?' I like to try and scare the hell out of everybody first and say, 'Okay, do you really believe this is what God's called you to do?' Because it is so tough, and it really is an endurance test. Just breaking in is very difficult, and then just staying in is very difficult."

Going back to a verse in the Bible grounds the journey both for Cunningham and his wife: "Be as shrewd as snakes and as innocent as doves" (Matthew 10:16). Cunningham said that even with this in mind, it's difficult to maintain respect. "How do you lead a set in a servant attitude without that being interpreted as weakness, in a business where people prey on weakness?" he asked rhetorically.

In playing the Hollywood game and getting very good at it, with his team of lawyers and agents in his corner, Cunningham questions whether or not that is the right game to play. He reports that he's had to deal with enough power plays and egos to know that making a difference in Hollywood means more than that. It comes down to seeking God, seeking wisdom, and picking your battles.

"It is a moment-by-moment walk, and it's not easy," he said. "That's why I really challenge young people and say, 'Are you sure?' If you're sure, I will bleed for you. I will give you everything that I know. I've facilitated dozens of interns over the years and try to be very generous with what I've learned the hard way, but don't waste my time. If you like movies, great, go to the movies. Watch *Entertainment Tonight* and pray. But if you come to the frontlines, then you better have the training; don't just show up. Do your homework. And you better be solid with your God, because it's going to be tested on a daily basis. And then, you better have something to say. Don't be just another one of these guys that shows up and wants to entertain."

The key to making it in Hollywood Cunningham-style is "bulldog tenacity." He doesn't pin his success on any particular film school or method of filmmaking—just the fact that he keeps trying to make movies. His advice to others is the same, whether they're making short films, wedding videos, commercials, music videos, or documentaries—just keep making films.

"Keep that momentum moving forward, because you will stall out, and you will ultimately end up doing something else if you don't keep moving forward," he said. "If you can't afford a film school, go on the web, and you'll learn a ton there. Become a sponge and become lethal and effective in that way. Don't come into it half-cocked. With that mentality, you will get there. And you'll meet people along the way that are smarter than you; you'll meet people along the way that have more resources than you; you'll meet people along the way that have better personalities that make them able to somehow know everybody and network. But you can outlast these people. And if you are called to this, it will happen. It may take you five years and fifteen, twenty years. But don't give up."

Note

1. *To End All Wars* production notes, *www.argyllfilms.com/reviews.html* (accessed July 26).

WRITER

LEE BATCHLER

Smoke & Mirrors — 2004
My Name is Modesty:
A Modesty Blaise Adventure — 2003
The Spittin' Image — 1997
Batman Forever — 1995

WRITER

JANET BATCHLER

Smoke & Mirrors — 2004
My Name is Modesty:
A Modesty Blaise Adventure — 2003
The Spittin' Image — 1997
Batman Forever — 1995

DIRECTOR

The Spittin' Image — 1997

10 LEE & JANET BATCHLER

⊠ THE MILLION DOLLAR $CRIPT

"I'm a Christian, and I've never been a writer without being a Christian. So I don't have anything to compare it to. The stories that we are attracted to are a function of who we are as people and as Christians. We tell certain stories, and we're not attracted to other stories."
—Janet Batchler

When Christian screenwriters Lee and Janet Scott Batchler decided to write the screenplay that would make their careers, the duo wanted to write a fastball—a page-turner that couldn't be put down. The husband and wife writing team, who had been writing kids' videos and low-budget films, starting searching for the idea that would set them apart from the pack, garner them notice in Hollywood, and, if all went well, get them work for years to come.

Usually, when writers sit down to craft a screenplay, they begin with an idea that they think will make a successful movie, and they dive into it with passion and intensity, but in truth, never expect much. The Batchlers attacked their script a bit differently, setting out to write the script that would put them on the map, period.

Less than two years later, the Batchlers sold their spec screenplay *Smoke and Mirrors* for a cool million dollars, and then, if that wasn't enough, Warner Brothers hired the husband and wife screenwriting team to write the third installment in the Batman franchise, *Batman Forever*, what some have called Warner Brothers' most valuable corporate asset of that time.

How does one set a goal like that and then achieve it so forcefully?

"We got to the point where we said it's time to really go for it and write a weekend read, which is a script that is sent home with an executive or a producer and must be read by Monday," Janet said. "We began to search for a great story that would be worth being a weekend read because we wanted to get noticed."[1]

The Batchlers began searching for the script idea in the early '90s, the one that would distinguish them from the hundreds of thousands of aspiring writers who roam Hollywood, cranking out thousands upon thousands of screenplays every year. Hollywood boasts a daunting and competitive field, but if a writer's got talent, it's only a matter of time.

Now, there are many film industry myths.

There's the myth that every person in Hollywood (and the greater Los Angeles area) has a script they're either writing or trying to sell. Despite the impossibility of this myth, it stems from the idea that everyone has an idea for a movie and is apt to tell you about it if they discover you work at a film studio or for a production company.

Then there's the myth of the million-dollar script: a piece of writing that is so sharp, well written, and commercially salable that it becomes a very hot property, very fast. This kind of script is often looked at as a kind lottery ticket for both the serious writers in town and those who are simply gold digging opportunists. In fact, this myth is one of the driving forces of the massive number of scripts that producers and studios are forced to sift through every day.

For Lee and Janet Batchler, the million-dollar script is no longer a myth.

SMOKE AND **MIRRORS**: WRITING THE WEEKEND READ

"A mediocre story, NO MATTER HOW MUCH YOU POLISH IT UP or how much skill you apply, will remain mediocre. A great story can often survive mediocre execution." —Lee Batchler[2]

Lee met Janet at a church game night. He was a musical writer and playwright, and she was a UCLA student. The two hit it off, got married, and then struck up an unlikely writing partnership that has lasted for years. "We thought, maybe we can do screenwriting," Janet said. "So I started writing in the very late '80s."

The Batchlers began searching for their script idea in the early '90s. The two writers belonged to a writers group that met every other week, which can be a vital part of any writer's life, by offering a safe space to bring writing and ideas and most importantly, receive honest feedback from others working on similar projects.

In this case, the Batchlers' writing group became their movie idea sounding board as they searched for the one that would become their next screenplay. Upon deciding that they were going to write an amazing script, the Batchlers brought four potential movie ideas to the group and pitched them one by one. And one by one, the group feedback was,

"That's not the one."

"The group leader told us to come back the following week with four more ideas," Janet said. "We came back with nine new ideas, most of which were garbage, but one was *Smoke and Mirrors*, which got us our first job."[3]

The script that got them their first job followed a nineteenth century magician by the name of Jean-Robert Houdin, who is best known as the man who invented the idea and practice of modern stage magic.

"The group all said, 'I haven't seen that before; we want to hear more about that," Janet said. So the two began to write *Smoke and Mirrors*.[4]

According to Janet, Houdin invented the rabbit out of the hat trick, the almost clichéd staple of modern stage magic now practiced world-wide. And while Houdin's story is a long one, the Batchlers decided to focus on one chapter from his book. That particular chapter centers on an episode of Houdin's post-retirement life that makes for a great action adventure story. The story picks up when Houdin retired and the French government asked him to go to Algeria to help quell an uprising of Berber sorcerers.

"There were these sorcerers doing magic out in the desert and trying to get people to rise up against the government. They thought themselves gods," Janet said. "Houdin was asked to go to Algeria to expose these sorcerers as fakes. He put on several shows for influential Frenchman, and then he was asked to go way out into the desert, basically have a one-on-one showdown at the palace of the most influential Arab Sheik."

In the true story, Houdin is purported to have met the main Sheik, who offers him a challenge. The Sheik tells Houdin, 'I hear that you can catch a bullet in your teeth. But I want you to do it with a bullet from my gun.' The Sheik pulls a gun and fires a bullet, and Houdin catches it in his teeth. In the story, Houdin goes home and retires.

But the Batchlers took their script to another level entirely. "Our third act becomes this massive set piece, set in an ancient fortress carved into the mountains," Janet said. "Our guys have to fight their way back home past a massive army led by the evil sorcerer, and they don't really have a lot available to them. We took [Houdin's] wife with him; we also gave them a foreign legionnaire character, because at that time, the foreign legion was brand new."

The trio of primary characters in the script version offered a chance for not just one or two big actors to attach themselves to the script, but three, and on top of that, the script featured a love triangle romance that complicated things even further. In some reports, the script, which hasn't been produced yet, follows Houdin and his wife, and in other reports, it follows Houdin and his young assistant and lover. Apparently the script went through a variety of writers after the Batchlers sold it.

The Batchlers wrote the script in 1992 and continued to polish it until it was absolutely ready to make the rounds at the studios. Even then, when they knew the script was at its best, they didn't send it out immediately. They took their time to make sure they had the story just right before they got ready to show anyone.

Soon, they handed it off to their agent, who immediately formed a unique strategy around selling the script. "Instead of sending it out, our agent went out himself and talked about it. He told executives the script was coming, and they didn't want to miss reading it," Lee said. "He waited and let the word spread. When he finally sent it out, he did so only to those who had the money to make it. So when the script did go out, executives were anxious to read it."[5]

Then the bidding war began.

When the script went out on a Tuesday afternoon, a number of major executives had been primed and readied. The Batchlers' agent, Alan Gasmer, had talked up the story as promised, and when Jay Stern, an executive at Disney's Hollywood Pictures, got a hold of it, he couldn't put it down.

As studios read the script, the heat began to rise.

By Friday, things had cranked up several notches, as Gasmer talked up the million-dollar number and the studios scrambled to make their bid. "They were in the middle of a bidding war when Bruce Berman, who was the head of Warner Brothers, got on a plane in New York," Janet said. "The plane was grounded because of a snowstorm, and people had been telling him to read our script, so he did and was determined to buy it."[6]

By Friday afternoon, Bruce Berman, the Warner Brothers executive who had to give the okay to purchase the script, was stuck on the tarmac at an airport in New York and couldn't use his phone.

Stern seized the opportunity to make the deal, and by the time Berman's plane was in the air and he was able to make a phone call, Stern delivered one million dollars for the Batchler's first script, and the deal was done.

During the bidding war, Lee and Janet were at a writers' retreat where, upon hearing the news, they celebrated by taking a group of writer friends out to dinner, in light of the fact that they were flat broke up until that moment.

Despite the furor over *Smoke and Mirrors*, which finally sold in 1993, the trip to the screen has still not officially taken place as of this writing. At various points, the film has had a number of different actors, writers, and directors attached to make it, including Sean Connery and Frank Marshall, director John McTiernan and later Mel Gibson, but it wasn't until almost eight years later that it almost happened. When Michael Douglas and Catherine Zeta-Jones expressed interest in the script (the two were hot off the critically acclaimed Steven Soderbergh film *Traffic*), the project jumped onto the fast track.

"They had a director attached, Mimi Leder, who directed *Deep Impact*," Janet said. "It was being prepped in 2001 to shoot in Morocco, and then

9/11 happened. It was gonna start within a few months, and then it got completely derailed. Given the global political climate, [it was] just not the right time."

And now the movie is on hold again, either sitting on the shelf or awaiting another round of attachments and casting decisions. "Every time we talk to our agent about it, he says this movie is going to get made," Janet said. "We just say that nobody has ruined a frame of it yet."

Once the bidding war for *Smoke and Mirrors* cooled down, Warner Brothers decided to go after the husband and wife writers. They began sending the duo potential writing projects, including *Lethal Weapon 4*, but the Batchlers turned down project after project, waiting for something that suited their tastes and styles.

BATMAN **FOREVER**

"Now there was always a bit of competition between the corporate offices of Warner Brothers and Disney, SO WARNER BROTHERS DECIDED IF WE CAN'T GET THE SCRIPT, LET'S GET THE WRITERS. So they started offering us projects, and we were turning them down because it just didn't appeal to us or we weren't right for the project."
—Janet Batchler

When Warner Brothers offered Lee and Janet the opportunity to write the third movie in the immensely popular *Batman* series, the writing team jumped at the chance and crafted the smart and dualistic *Batman Forever*, the film that saw the *Batman* franchise hit its peak in popularity before bombing out later with *Batman and Robin*.

The most interesting aspect of *Batman Forever* is its treatment of each character as having two faces or two different lives. It is a theme that permeates nearly every major character in the film: Batman and Bruce Wayne, Two-Face and Harvey Dent, Riddler and Edward Nygma, Robin and Dick Grayson. These unique parallel lives coexisting represent the two sides to each character—the normal, everyday personality and the alter ego, all of whom are either superheroes or super-villains. It's a very interesting commentary on a fantasy that many "normal" people have to either be very bad or very good, even while living normal lives.

The Batchlers take this fascination with dueling personalities a step beyond the previous *Batman* movies by playing it up in every possible instance. Two-Face is the most literal example of this, as his two personalities coexist at all times; even his hideout is split into two sides: one side representing a suave, debonair socialite-type, the other side representing the crazed criminal. He even has two girlfriends, Sugar and Spice, one for each of his personalities.

Batman Forever, like *Batman* and *Batman Returns*, also finds a resonant theme in the idea of vigilante justice that often forms the basis of comic book and superhero stories. This theme struck a chord with *MovieGuide*'s Ted Baehr, who called *Batman Forever* "a strong morality tale written by two Christians who are actively involved in Christian ministry in Hollywood."[7]

Batman Forever isn't a powerhouse of spiritual film; it's an over-the-top powerhouse popcorn film and an example of two Christians working at the absolute top of their craft, gaining further influence and respect in Hollywood as a result.

HOLLYWOOD CHRISTIANS

"We work a lot on our stories. We mete out our stories in great detail, we make sure WE UNDERSTAND WHO OUR CHARACTERS are, and WE MAKE SURE OF OUR STORY. Then we go off into separate offices and work on separate parts of the movie." —Janet Batchler

The Batchlers continue to keep a full writing schedule as they have finished up several projects involving the character of Modesty Blaise, who is often described as the female James Bond. In addition, they have written a script for Disney titled *The Shores of Tripoli*, which is set to hit theaters in 2005.

In humorously referring to their writing relationship and the joys of working with a screenwriting partner, Lee said, "Ya know, she got gaps, I got gaps. We fill in each others' gaps."

The husband and wife writing team also keep busy speaking at Christian conferences and events that pertain to entertainment and faith, while both of them are instructors at the Christian writing program, Act One: Screenwriting for Hollywood. In the past few years, they have also lectured at the USC Film School, UC San Diego, Biola University, the Scriptwriter's Network, Women in Film, and the Writer's Connection. Janet is also a juror for the Damah Film Festival, an annual event she feels is having a very positive impact, where short films dealing with spiritual issues compete in a typical film festival competition. "It's a cool festival in part because it focuses on shorts, and it focuses on people who are trying to say something that doesn't always get said; they're approaching Hollywood in a way that isn't always approached."

As writers, the Batchlers have a lot to say on the subject of what it takes to succeed in Hollywood as a screenwriter. Janet talks openly about how Christian screenwriters, and most aspiring screenwriters, simply need to study screenwriting and take their time to learn the craft to become better writers.

"No one wants to fail," she said. "It takes very hard work to get good enough so they don't ignore you. It seems that the non-believers in the business recognize this principle more than we do."

And according to the Batchlers, there are three keys to success and, more importantly, survival in Hollywood: excellence, wisdom, and contentment—excellence so people can't ignore your work, wisdom in order to do business in a cutthroat industry, and contentment so that if you never sell that script or never win an Oscar, you can still live your life and be content.

When it comes to movies that have a spiritual agenda, Janet is quick to call a spade a spade. "Most 'Christian' movies today fall under the definition of propaganda, and frankly, most people don't really want to watch propaganda," Janet said. "That doesn't mean Christianity has no place in movies."

To prove her point, Janet cites Tim McCanlies' film *The Iron Giant* as a successful story that portrays the Gospel message through a moving metaphor and a relationship between a boy and an alien robot.

But is there another calling in the works for one of the Batchlers? In 1997, Janet participated in a directing workshop for women at the American Film Institute. During her time at the institute, Janet made a short film called *The Spitting Image*, an experience that gave her a feeling that she had found her calling.

"I felt like I found what I was really meant to do," she said. "It's very hard for women to be seen and protected as directors. If that's something that doesn't ever happen, I have to be okay with that. I have other things in my life. But I would not feel comfortable neglecting my husband, my kids, and my writing."

Who knows what will come next from the husband and wife writing team, but for now, they're content to keep on writing.

Notes

1. Frederic T. Dray, "How a Husband and Wife Achieved Screenwriting Success," *Script* magazine, April 22, 2003. Online at *www.scriptmag.com/articles/view_article.php?id=213* (accessed 2004).

2. Ibid.

3. Ibid.

4. Ibid.

5. Ibid.

6. Thom Taylor, *The Big Deal: Hollywood's Million Dollar Spec Script Market*, excerpted at *www.absolutewrite.com/screenwriting/million_dollar_script.htm* (accessed May 14, 2004).

7. John Dart, "Hollywood Gets Religion?" online at Milligan.edu. *www.milligan.edu/communications/Library/Articles1/holywd.htm* (accessed July 26, 2004).

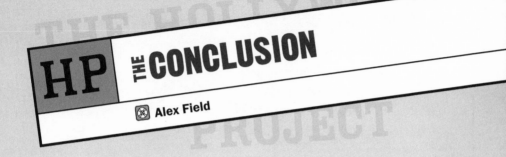

HP ᴛʜᴇ CONCLUSION

⊗ Alex Field

> "I know that all over the world there are young people borrowing from relatives and saving their allowances to buy their first cameras and put together their first student movies, some of them dreaming of becoming famous and making a fortune. But a few are dreaming of finding out what matters to them, of saying to themselves and to anyone who will listen, "I care." A few of them want to make good movies."[1]
>
> --Sidney Lumet, *Making Movies*

In the home where I grew up, there was always a small war over the VCR. My mother often decided which movies to censor for the entire household, and my father basically decided which movies to uncensor for the entire household.

Our movie watching diet was mildly oriented toward action movies, while my two brothers and I often scoffed at period dramas, romances, and the like. I remember the day my parents and some of their friends decided to watch all four hours of *Gone With the Wind* on one long weekend afternoon. While we lamented this fact in the backyard, in our rooms, and while tinkering around in the garage, I was overjoyed the moment that overwrought and overly dramatic (to my young mind) southern epic ended.

Despite the occasional battles over the films we watched, my siblings and I still managed to get in front of *Star Wars* early on and its inevitable sequels soon after. In fact, we were all Arnold Schwarzenegger action movie fans at a young age. That gives you an idea of the decade in which I grew up.

Through this, I came to see film as something important, something that could influence people, especially young people, and, whether I realized it then or not, something, not unlike other major strands of pop culture, that had the power to change a person's life on any number of levels.

While my taste in the kinds of movies I watch has evolved over the years and continues to change even today, my respect for them has not.

Somewhere in between weekend movie-watching marathons and heading off down the street to the bargain theater on Saturday nights, I came to love movies. Perhaps it was inherent in my personality that I would become enraptured by the joy of escaping into another's milieu; maybe it came from my love for writing stories or reading science fiction novels and *Narnia*-esque fantasy.

I think it might be true that everyone is drawn to movies, although each of us is compelled by different characters, stories, genres, and styles that seem, somehow, to be unique to our own story.

This book was meant for film lovers and, I think, for those who might have wanted to learn something from those breaking down barriers in the film industry and making films because they care, because that story, that character, or that subject mattered to them.

Unfortunately, we will probably still see films come out that are aesthetically hard to watch or seem to misrepresent the Gospel and everything that the Church stands for. But it's a free country, and the filmmaker to blame for those failures could very well be directing tomorrow's blockbusters. There are a great many lessons still to be learned about the art of making a powerful spiritual film.

Some brief cases in point: In his introduction to his screenplay for *Magnolia*, Paul Thomas Anderson discusses the merits of writing from the gut, which helped give *Magnolia* amazing force (he calls the film a study in writing from the gut); and he also discusses the power of writing to music.[2] Robert Rodriguez, the famed writer/director of *Desperado*, *Once Upon a Time in Mexico* and the *Spy Kids* trilogy, says to skip film school, "work hard and be scary."[3] Filmmaker and actor Edward Burns echoes the film school sentiment, saying that "no school can teach you to be passionate or give you a vision or give you the guts to keep writing scripts when the rejection letters keep piling up."[4] Filmmaker and actor John Cassavetes says this: "Anyone who can make a film, I already love. But I feel sorry if they don't put any thought in it because then they missed the boat. As an artist, I feel that we must try many things—but above all, we must dare to fail. You must have the courage to be bad—to be willing to risk everything to really express it all."[5]

But the most powerful lesson that I learned after researching, interviewing filmmakers, and writing this book is that culture is being transformed by film today in a number of very unique and exciting ways. Filmmakers are charging onto the film scene and influencing culture in colorful brush strokes through the films they make and the people they interact with, and each of them is doing it in a distinctive way.

For filmmakers, it's also interesting to discover that there is no specific road to Hollywood that is marked by directions or road signs. In the same way that the innumerable truths of the Bible pull at each of us in personal ways, perhaps then, as we have seen in this book, each filmmaker will pursue God through film based on his or her own individual experiences. Put simply, there is no map to succeeding in the film world. The important thing is just to make movies.

Film is a medium that can be used uniquely and individually to further the body of Christ. As Jesus used parables and grand metaphors, to reveal truth to people when He walked the earth, how much more so should we be passionate about sharing the truths of scripture with people through film?

Mel Gibson's *Braveheart* is one of my favorite films—it has made my ever-shuffling top ten list several times. The day I watched Braveheart for the first time, I remember walking out of the darkened movie theater into a foggy afternoon in Southern California, feeling absolutely stunned. The day looked different, my heart was pounding—the movie had gotten underneath my skin. I remember thinking about the passion of William Wallace and wanting to bottle that power, capture it, or adopt it as my own. It was sometime later, after watching Gibson's epic again and again, that I realized that Gibson had done just that: He had bottled the passion of this man's life onscreen, and he had used it to influence his audience, to evoke emotion, and to bring a powerful message of hope.

I don't walk out of a movie theater feeling that way very often, but in the few times that it has happened, I walk away with a renewed respect for the power of the movies. In the end, and this is now the end, whether you are watching movies, analyzing movies, writing movies, directing movies, producing movies, or some combination of these, God will use even the least of us to make the most powerful changes in our culture. And don't underestimate the power of film.

Notes

1. Sidney Lumet, *Making Movies* (New York: Vintage Books, 1996) p. 47.
2. Paul Thomas Anderson, *Magnolia* (New York: Newmarket Press, 2000) p. vii.
3. Robert Rodriguez, *Rebel Without a Crew* (New York: Plume Books, 1996) n.p.
4. Edward Burns, *Three Screenplays by Edward Burns* (Hyperion, 1998) p 3.
5. John Cassavetes, quoted at IndustryCentral.com. *www.industrycentral.net/director_interviews/JO-HCAS01.HTM* (accessed August 9, 2004).

HP THE MOVIE LIST

⊠ Spiritually Intriguing Films

The following less-than-comprehensive and entirely subjective list of film descriptions detail some of the more spiritually intriguing films available (in addition to the films discussed in this book). Please do not consider this list a blind recommendation, as you may find some of these films inappropriate based on your personal convictions. But many, if not all of them, have the ability to inspire much conversation. In no particular order:

THE **APOSTLE**

(Rated PG-13, 1997, Directed by Robert Duvall)

One of the more powerful and conflicted spiritual films in the last decade, Robert Duvall's *The Apostle* brings up many interesting questions regarding evangelism, fallibility, and forgiveness.

THE **MISSION**

(Rated PG, 1986, Directed by Roland Joffe)

The Mission stars Robert DeNiro and Jeremy Irons and depicts the struggle of a pair of Spanish Jesuit priests as they seek to help and minister to a South American Indian tribe.

THE **COUNT** OF **MONTE CRISTO**

(Rated PG-13, 2002, Directed by Kevin Reynolds)

The classic story is retold in a redemptive way that warrants a closer look. With two solid lead actors, Jim Caviezel and Guy Pearce, this film is a story of betrayal, redemption, and ultimately, revenge, which creates an interesting tension from beginning to end.

LUTHER

(Rated PG-13, 2003, Directed by Eric Till)

An independent film released to little notice or acclaim, *Luther* is a very interesting film about Martin Luther, the man who stood up to the Catholic Church and wrote up his 95 Theses, or disagreements with Catholic traditions and dogma. Starring Joseph Fiennes in a unique and moving performance.

SIGNS

(Rated PG-13, 2002, Directed by M. Night Shyamalan)

M. Night Shyamalan's summer blockbuster is about aliens that invade earth after a rash of crop circles appear around the world. But this movie also follows a former minister, played by Mel Gibson, who has lost his faith in God.

THE BIG **KAHUNA**

(Rated R, 1999, Directed by John Swanbeck)

Based on the play *Hospitality Suite*, written by Roger Rueff, *The Big Kahuna* could be called a non-Christian's view of evangelism. Despite bad language, this film (featuring tour de force performances from Kevin Spacey, Danny Devito, and Peter Facinelli), contains very moving dialogue, wonderful lingering stories, and a few lessons as well.

MAGNOLIA

(Rated R, 1999, Directed by Paul Thomas Anderson)

This ensemble film features a kaleidoscope of colorful characters (and some really offensive characters) and finds its power in the themes of guilt and forgiveness. *Magnolia* is sweet and hard-hitting, poignant and repugnant, startling and powerful.

WAKING THE DEAD

(Rated R, 2000, Directed by Keith Gordon)

Waking the Dead is a powerful indie film that drives home the dual themes of love and doing what you think is right. This haunting film, with a style all its own, sees Billy Crudup give a stunning, career-making performance.

BABETTE'S FEAST

(Rated G, 1987, Directed by Gabriel Axel)

This film is a treat for those with a love for all things culinary; *Babette's Feast* is a lovely tale about puritanical religion, devotion, joy, hospitality, and kindness.

FEARLESS

(Rated R, 1993, Directed by Peter Weir)

Peter Weir's little seen but rousing drama follows a man who survives a plane crash and feels as if he's invulnerable. Jeff Bridges and Rosie Perez shine in emotionally intense performances.

THE **BELIEVER**

(Rated R, 2003, Directed by Henry Bean)

A violent and shocking story of a young Jewish teenager with loads of charisma who develops an anti-Semitic worldview while wrestling with his heritage. *The Believer* is a film about faith, God, free will, and one man's struggle in the midst of a strange situation. Ryan Gosling confirms his massive talent in this paradoxical role.

CHANGING LANES

(Rated R, 2002, Directed by Roger Michell)

This dramatic thriller is a unique film starring Ben Affleck and Samuel L. Jackson that ponders the limits of a person's capacity for revenge and forgiveness.

BRAVE**HEART**

(Rated R, 1995, Directed by Mel Gibson)

Mel Gibson's Academy Award–winning Scottish epic is a story that, on a base level, has everything going for it: There's tension, there's romance, there's political scheming, there's drama, there's a man overcoming great odds; and the battle scenes are the greatest since *Spartacus* (1960).

BRUCE ALMIGHTY

(Rated PG-13, 2003, Directed by Tom Shadyac)

Jim Carrey spoofs God but maintains near-Christian theology throughout this movie (if you can get past the whole man becomes God for a month plotline). *Bruce Almighty* tries to allow viewers to see the world as God sees it (and as Jim Carrey might see it).

STAR **WARS**

(Rated PG, 1977, Directed by George Lucas)

This film has served as a touchstone and pop culture phenomenon since its release. But though *Star Wars* is a spiritual fantasy story, it treats religion as simplistic dualism.

BEN-HUR

(Rated G, 1959, Directed by William Wyler)

I avoided watching this film for many years because I thought it was about a charioteer named Ben. It's not, as I'm sure many of you know. This is an amazing film about Jesus and probably one of the great epic movies ever made.

DONNIE **DARKO**

(Rated R, 2001, Directed by Richard Kelly)

Richard Kelly's spooky and playful dramatic science fiction teen spiritual thriller embodies genre-defiance and takes some time to sort out after the credits roll. The story careens from destruction to self-discovery, selfishness to self-sacrifice, interchangeably.

THE **SHAWSHANK** REDEMPTION

(Rated R, 1994, Directed by Frank Darabont)

Tim Robbins and Morgan Freeman star in one of the best films of the '90s. *The Shawshank Redemption* is almost universally loved because it mines the themes of hope and friendship to great effect, even though it takes place in a jail.

FIGHT CLUB

(Rated R, 1999, Directed by David Fincher)

Prepare for a wild, sometimes confusing ride. *Fight Club,* with this gritty and brutal look at the disillusionment of the postmodern mindset, presents issues, seeks answers, and shares some valuable insights that might take some time to absorb, and then discuss.

DOGMA

(Rated R, 1999, Directed by Kevin Smith)

Kevin Smith's *Dogma* is an irreverent, raucous, and witty film that pokes fun at religion, nuns, the Bible, and God in a good-natured, though at times, off-color way. The film features actors Ben Affleck, Matt Damon, Chris Rock, Salma Hayek, and Linda Fiorentino.

21 GRAMS

(Rated R, 2003, Directed by Alejandro Gonzales Inarittu)

21 Grams features outstanding performances from Benicio del Toro, Sean Penn, and Naomi Watts. The editing is purposefully fragmented, but the style only serves to intensify the story of flawed characters seeking love and coping with loss.

WHALE RIDER

(Rated G, 2002, Directed by Niki Caro)

This quiet independent movie hits with little or no warning, starting slow and building fast, into one of the more fascinating portraits of spirituality in recent memory.

Alex Field is a twenty-seven-year-old writer and editor from Southern California, where he lives with his wife, Nicole, and sons, Ari and Elijah. He is currently an associate editor for Gospel Light Publications in Ventura, California.

Prior to working with Gospel Light, Field was the executive director of Epic Ministries, the nonprofit, sister organization to the world-renowned Skate Street Skatepark, where he edited a regional skateboarding and punk rock magazine, ran a music venue, and promoted school assemblies, outreach events, and concerts. As an MPAA accredited freelance writer, Field has written and reported for the *Los Angeles Times*, the Associated Press, *RES* magazine, *The Ventura Independent*, *The VC Reporter*, and he is a regular contributor to both RELEVANT magazine and *Outreach* magazine, among other outlets.

[RELEVANTBOOKS]

FOR MORE INFORMATION ABOUT OTHER RELEVANT BOOKS,
CHECK OUT WWW.RELEVANTBOOKS.COM.